Healing Ourselves,
Empowering Ourselves

Healing Ourselves, Empowering Ourselves

Women Creating Ritual

Barbara J. Des Marais

VANTAGE PRESS
New York

Published by Vantage Press, Inc.
516 West 34th Street, New York, New York 10001

Manufactured in the United States of America
ISBN: 0-533-11216-8

Library of Congress Catalog Card No.: 94-90370

0 9 8 7 6 5 4 3 2 1

To my great, great, great, great, great-grandmothers

Contents

List of Tables   ix
Acknowledgments   xi
Preface   xiii

I. INTRODUCTION   1
    Statement of the Problem   1
    Statement of Research Questions   2
    Definition of Key Terms   2
II. REVIEW OF RELATED LITERATURE   6
    Anthropological and Historical Literature   6
    Contemporary Literature   8
    Cross-Cultural Literature   13
    Framework for This Study   14
    Literature Summary   18
III. RESEARCH METHODS   21
    Subjects   21
    Research Methods   21
    Questionnaire   22
    Interview   22
IV. RESULTS AND DISCUSSION   24
    Characteristics of Women in the Ritual
        Groups   24
    Characteristics of the Ritual Groups   29
    Characteristics of Women's Ritual   41
    Roots and Sources of the Groups' Rituals   50
    Growth Prospects   52
    Relationship to the Women's Movement   64

V. CONCLUSION   70
        The Ritual Framework and Women's Ritual   70
        Summary of the Study   77

APPENDICES
Appendix A. Cover Letter and Survey
        Questionnaire for This Study   83
Appendix B. Interview Schedule for This Study   88

Endnotes   99
Bibliography   101

List of Tables

1. Age Distribution of Respondents   26
2. Annual Income of Respondents   27

Acknowledgments

I wish to thank Diane Schaffer. Her time, energy, support, feedback, optimism, and sense of humor were enormously valuable and important to me in the process of completing this text. Also, I thank Meg Bowman and Barbara Dubins. To Meg, much appreciation for her support, references, and experience with women's ritual. Much appreciation to Barbara for all her support. It was Barbara's words, "It doesn't have to be perfect; it just has to be done," that kept me writing at times when I didn't think I could write another word.

Finally, I wish to thank all the women who participated in this study. Without their cooperation it could not have been made.

Preface

In April 1987 I completed my master's thesis. It was titled *Characteristics of Women's Ritual in the San Francisco Bay Area.* Since I completed my thesis, I have watched the women's spirituality movement continue to grow and reach more and more women.

After receiving positive feedback from those who've read my thesis, especially from my friend, Yvonne Quevedo, I decided the research and information in my thesis could be valuable to those interested in women's spirituality and women's ritual. This book includes a discussion of literature about women's spirituality, especially some of the earliest works on this subject. In addition, this book includes information taken directly from women who practice women's spirituality and women's ritual, including: how it is practiced; group dynamics; and spiritual experiences and growth as a result of creating and practicing women's ritual.

Therefore, I offer this book as a resource to all those interested in women's spirituality and especially to those interested in women's ritual. I hope you enjoy reading it and using it as much as I enjoyed researching it and writing it.

Barbara Des Marais
August 1994

Healing Ourselves,
Empowering Ourselves

CHAPTER I
Introduction

Statement of the Problem

Since the second wave of the women's movement began in the United States in the 1960s, several branches and expressions of the women's movement have evolved. These include Marxist feminism, radical feminism, eco-feminism, and spiritual feminism, among others. Spiritual feminism, also known as women's spirituality or feminist spirituality, has been growing since the 1970s. Women are reclaiming women-centered spiritual traditions and/or creating alternative women-centered spiritual groups. A primary expression of women's spirituality is women's ritual.

To date there has been no systematic study of the various loosely organized women's ritual groups. This text is an exploratory study of this growing part of the women's movement. It describes and analyzes women's ritual in the San Francisco Bay Area. The description and analysis are based on a study of five Bay Area ritual groups. Specifically, this study examines the characteristics of women practicing ritual, describes the nature of, or content of, women's ritual as practiced in the San Francisco Bay Area in the 1980s, and discusses the possibilities for future growth of women's ritual.

In order to narrow the focus of this study, spiritual feminists and women's ritual groups within organized

1

Judeo-Christian religious traditions are specifically excluded.

Statement of Research Questions

The following questions guided the design of this study:

1. What are the characteristics of women who participate in women's ritual groups in the San Francisco Bay Area?
2. What is their definition of women's ritual and how women's ritual is practiced?
3. What are the prospects for the growth of women's ritual in the San Francisco Bay Area?
4. Is there a relationship between participation in women's ritual and participation in other forms of the women's movement?

Definition of Key Terms

Key terms used in this thesis include the following: social movement, feminist spirituality, women's ritual, and women's ritual groups. Discussed below are definitions of these terms, as used in this study.

Social Movement

According to *A Modern Dictionary of Sociology, social movement* is defined as:

An important form of Collective Behavior in which large numbers of people are organized or alerted to support and bring about or to resist social change. Revolutions and reformations are general types of social movements. Participation in a social movement is for most people only informal or indirect. Usually large numbers of sympathizers identify with and support the movement and its program without joining any formal organizations associated with the movement.[1]

For purposes of this study, the term *social movement* varies slightly from this standard definition. In particular, the number of women who participate in women's ritual in the San Francisco Bay Area may not be regarded as "large numbers." Also, in this study, many who identify with the women's ritual movement have "joined" their ritual group. In addition, each group may not necessarily be regarded as a "formal organization" but is regarded as associated with the women's ritual movement. Finally, the term *women's ritual movement*, as used in this study, is understood to be not a movement by itself; rather, it is a part of or offshoot of the larger women's movement.

Feminist Spirituality

In her book *Moon, Moon*, Anne Kent Rush defines *feminist spirituality* as "the process of integration, of connection. [It] is not focused on transcending everyday life but on recognizing the power in it. It is also not focused on 'transcending the self or the ego,' but on integrating one's ego-self with the collective self."[2]

This is the definition used for this study. However, not

3

all of the interviewees in this study agree with this definition. (See chapter IV for the interviewees' variations.)

Also, for purposes of this study, *religion* means an
organized group with a system of beliefs and practices. In
addition, *religious* means the practice of and subscribing
to the beliefs of a religion. Therefore, *spiritual* shall be
distinct from *religious* in that one may be spiritual without
aligning with a religion. (Again, see chapter IV for variations
in this definition as reported by the interviewees in this
study.)

Ritual

According to the *Abingdon Dictionary of Living Religions:*

> Ritual is one of the oldest, most complex, and persistent
> symbolic activities associated with religion. Ritual is a para-
> digm and dramatization of the intent of religion itself; it
> marshals visual and aural symbols along with intellectual
> and sensual images into a process that provides a partici-
> pant with a certain identity and a sense of transformation
> into a new mode of being. In what is seen, said, and done,
> ritual expresses the psychic, social, and religious world of
> its participants even while inviting reflection on the cosmic
> significance of those known and ordered structures of ex-
> istence.[3]

This definition is basically followed in this text. The
only exception is in regard to the term religion. Many of
those participating in this study do not consider their
groups "religious," nor are they necessarily affiliated with
any particular "religion." However, all the interviewees
regard their groups as spiritual. Therefore, for this study,

4

spirituality replaces *religion* and *spiritual* replaces *religious* in the above definition of *ritual*.

Women's Ritual

For purposes of this study, *women's ritual* is ritual, according to the preceding definition of ritual, in which only women participate.

Women's Ritual Group

In this study, *women's ritual group* is defined as three or more women who meet specifically to perform women's ritual.

Finally, the term *Bay Area* will be used to mean San Francisco Bay Area.

CHAPTER II
Review of Related Literature

Literature centered on women's spirituality has grown rapidly in the last ten years. These works have influenced the growth and shape of women's ritual. The literature encompasses many perspectives, including anthropological, historical, contemporary, and cross-cultural perspectives.

Anthropological and Historical Literature

Merlin Stone, Margaret Murray, and Matilda Joslyn Gage have written books exploring pre-Christian spiritual traditions in Western cultures. The spiritual traditions of these cultures are being reclaimed by many in women's ritual groups.

For women's ritual it is significant that these cultures once existed and had powerful role models and images for women in the form of goddesses. In women's ritual these images are referenced in order that participants may emulate them and feel empowered as women.

One of the first to reinterpret anthropological findings from a feminist perspective was Merlin Stone. Her book *When God Was a Woman* was one of the earlier works in the contemporary women's movement, spawning interest in women's spirituality. First published in 1976, Stone's work drew on archaeological evidence to explore prepatriarchal cultures. In particular, Stone examined the cultures of the Near and Middle East. She described early women-centered cultures whose religion she referred to as "the Goddess religion."[1]

As interest in women's spirituality and prepatriarchal cultures grew, older works, previously discarded or disregarded, were sought out and reexamined for information they could contribute.

Margaret Murray's books were among these older works. In 1921, Murray wrote *The Witch-Cult in Western Europe*, and in 1931, *The God of the Witches*. In these books Murray discussed the pre-Christian cultures in Western Europe. In particular, Murray discussed the traditions and spirituality of these cultures. The spiritual traditions of the cultures examined in Murray's books are reflected in women's ritual.

Another early writer on this subject, whose work had been largely disregarded, was Matilda Joslyn Gage. Her book *Woman, Church and State* was first published in 1893. In the preface of her book, Gage wrote that she knew statements perpetuated by the church and state regarding the nature and role of women were false. She spent twenty years investigating these falsehoods. *Woman, Church and State* refutes the church and state's definition of woman, her nature, and her function in society. Gage studied and wrote about prepatriarchal societies where women were not oppressed but, rather, held positions of power and authority. She continued her study through the Christian takeover of Western Europe.

Gage's book brought to light many events that brought pre-Christian Western Europe to a close and resulted in deaths of up to 9 million people, most of them women, accused as witches. Gage described pre-Christian cultures in Europe and wrote how the Christian church systematically destroyed these cultures with greatest force from the fourteenth through the seventeenth centuries.[2] Gage's work has helped shape women's spirituality and women's ritual by providing evidence that women held positions of power and authority in prepatriarchal cultures. In this study, women's ritual draws on the traditions of these cultures. (See chapter IV.)

Contemporary Literature

The first compilation of works from the full spectrum of spiritual feminism is *Womanspirit Rising*. This is an anthology of writings on women's spirituality edited by Carol P. Christ and Judith Plaskow. In this book several spiritual feminists write about creating a spirituality that speaks to them as women. These women are creating their own spirituality by researching the roots of their spirituality, by telling their own personal stories as women, and by creating rituals. Among the authors in this book who are researching their roots is Merlin Stone. Her research indicates that archaeologists "traced the worship of the Goddess back to the Neolithic communities of about 70,000 B.C., some to the Upper Paleolithic cultures of about 25,000 B.C."[3] Stone further states that goddesses have been worshiped in all areas of the world.[4]

From this ancient base, many spiritual feminists are creating a new woman-centered Goddess spirituality. Carol Christ suggests one of the reasons women today seek the Goddess is that:

The symbol of Goddess has much to offer women who are struggling to be rid of the "powerful, pervasive, and long-lasting moods and motivations" of devaluation of female power, denigration of the female body, distrust of female will, and denial of the women's bonds and heritage that have been engendered by patriarchal religion. As women struggle to create a new culture in which women's power, bodies, will, and bonds are celebrated, it seems natural that the Goddess would re-emerge as symbol of the newfound beauty, strength, and power of women.[5]

Many participants in women's ritual look to images of the Goddess for just the reasons listed by Christ. The symbol of the Goddess offers women powerful affirmation of their womanselves.

After these earlier works, a number of books, journals, and essays were published in the late 1970s and continue to be published in the 1980s on the subject of women's spirituality. Many of these works focus on women's ritual as a central theme.

An in-depth examination of women's ritual is provided in an essay by Kay Turner, titled "Contemporary Feminist Ritual." In this essay Turner explores the reasons for and the effects of feminist rituals. She writes: "Successful and enduring changes in the status of women will come only through the parallel transformation of symbols and realities. Feminist ritual practice is currently the most important model for symbolic and, therefore, psychic and spiritual change in women."[6]

Turner identifies five key elements of women's ritual. These are: providing powerful female images, creating sacred space, female bonding, self-transformation, and commitment to societal transformation. Along with Christ and Stone, Turner affirms the need for the Goddess. According to Turner: "The suppression of the Goddess in our culture has meant the loss of images which identify personal and collective power in the female."[7]

In addition to providing strong female images, ritual provides a safe place or a sacred space for women to meet together. Turner writes about this sacred space stating: "Women are creating a space in which to feel better, to feel more, to feel the past as well as the future."[8]

Also very significant in women's ritual is "the importance of ritual as a formalized consecration of female bonding."[9] Turner stresses the importance in ritual of female bonding, of providing powerful female images, and of creating a space for women to feel safe and positive about themselves as women.

However, as significant as these aspects are in women's ritual, it may be that the most important aspect of ritual is the self-transformation of the participants. Regarding this, Turner writes:

> . . . the ritual space and activity are sacred in the sense of representing the possibilities of self-transformation. Part of the power and the fear experienced in ritual is the realization that one may change, become ultimately different, as a result of the experience or that the experience may suddenly make recognizable change that has been slowly rising from the depths of the personality.[10]

In addition to this self-transformation, Turner states: "The use of ritual is significant as a source for the renewal of commitment to evolving and transforming society as a whole."[11] Turner concludes that "ritual makes the ultimate ideal of relationship between self and community, the fusion, rather than separation, of these two direct realities."[12] These themes that Turner presents will be discussed in chapter IV as they are reflected in the responses of the practitioners of women's ritual studied for this text.

Two other contemporary authors, well known in

women's ritual circles, are Z. Budapest and Starhawk. Both women live in the Bay Area and have written books on women's spirituality and ritual.

Z. Budapest's books include *The Holy Book of Women's Mysteries: Part I* and *The Holy Book of Women's Mysteries: Part II*. Her books provide some background in women's history, particularly women's spiritual history. But the main focus of Budapest's books is women's rituals. In her books, she gives an abundance of practical guides for performing women's rituals. Budapest identifies herself as a witch. She was born in Hungary and was taught Hungarian witchcraft by her mother. The rituals in Budapest's books are those she has created using her family's traditions in combination with her feminist consciousness. She also includes rituals in her books that were developed by other spiritual feminists.

Starhawk has written *The Spiral Dance*, which offers background in what she refers to as the "Old Religion" of Europe. This is the pre-Christian religion of Europe. Starhawk also describes a variety of rituals, their significance, and how to perform them. She created these rituals after years of studying the history and practice of the old religion of Western Europe. Starhawk has also written *Dreaming the Dark*. In this book she discusses the use of ritual in conjunction with political activism to bring about social change.

Another guide for creating and practicing women's ritual is Hallie Iglehart's book *Womanspirit*. In this book, Iglehart writes of her own experience with ritual and delves into the significance of women's spirituality and ritual. She also offers practical guides for creating ritual. In discussing why women need to create their own rituals, Iglehart states: "Patriarchal ritual, in the form of many traditional religious services and patriotic holidays, is relatively dead as a spiritual experience. It is cut off from two essential aspects of ritual—spontaneous creative psychic power, and the cycles of nature."[13]

According to Iglehart: " ... the ultimate purpose of ritual is to learn to spontaneously create your own, according to the needs of the time and place. ... "[14] In addition, she says: "Every ritual is different, and the most important rule is to create a structure in which you can be spontaneous ...."[15] Iglehart then continues in her book to offer practical methods for creating ritual. She does this while pointing out the need for ritual to be creative, spontaneous, and to speak to the participants' needs.

The suggestions, guidelines, and influences of Budapest's, Starhawk's, and Iglehart's works are readily observed in the characteristics of the rituals practiced by the five groups studied for this thesis. (See chapter IV.)

Finally, among the contemporary works is a quarterly journal titled *Womanspirit*. *Womanspirit* was published from 1975 to 1984 by Jean and Ruth Mountaingrove. These journals provided women practicing ritual a wealth of information in women's religious history, current practices and rituals, and related poetry, music, and other artistic expressions. Another service these publications provided was a network among women in ritual. This network included not only women of the United States but extended to include women from many countries around the world.

In addition to these contemporary works on women's spirituality, several feminist magazines have featured women's spirituality. Charlene Spretnak notes in her anthology *The Politics of Women's Spirituality*: "In recent years nearly every major feminist magazine has featured an issue on women's spirituality, e.g., *Heresies: A Feminist Publication on Art and Politics*, no. 5; *Chrysalis: A Magazine of*

12

Women's Culture, no. 6; and *Quest: A Feminist Quarterly*, vol. 1, no. 4 and vol. 4, no. 3."[16]

More recently, *Ms.* magazine devoted most of its December 1985 issue to the topic of women's spirituality. Seven of the nine feature articles in this issue of *Ms.* were about women's spirituality.

Cross-Cultural Literature

Women's ritual draws on many cultural traditions. Recently, women of other cultural traditions have begun writing about women's spirituality and/or women's ritual in relation to their cultures.

Among these cross-cultural works related to women's spirituality and to women's ritual are two books published in 1985. The first is *Jambalaya: The Natural Woman's Book of Personal Charms and Practical Rituals.* This was written by Bay Area author Luisah Teish. In this book, Teish begins with her personal story, being brought up in Louisiana and learning from elder women the practices of her West African and Caribbean spiritual heritage commonly known, and often maligned, as Voodoo. Teish delves into the roots of the negative press around her ancestors' religion and describes the important role women played in this religion and in the culture in general. She also describes various rituals, their purposes, and how to perform them.

The second new cross-cultural work is *The Sacred Hoop: Recovering the Feminine in American Indian Traditions*, by Paula Gunn Allen. Allen identifies herself as an American Indian lesbian and in her book she describes how white, patriarchal colonizers distorted and nearly destroyed her culture. Concerning this, Allen writes:

During the five hundred years of Anglo-European colonization, the tribes have seen a progressive shift from gynecentric, egalitarian, ritual-based social systems to secularized structures closely imitative of the European patriarchal system. During this time women (including lesbians) and gay men—along with traditional medicine people, holy people, shamans, and ritual leaders—have suffered severe loss of status, power, and leadership. That these groups have suffered concurrent degradation is not coincidental; the woman-based, woman-centered traditions of many precontact tribes were tightly bound to ritual, and ritual was based on spiritual understandings rather than on economic or political ones. The genocide practiced against the tribes is aimed systematically at the dissolution of ritual tradition.[17]

From this, Allen makes a connection between the dissolution of ritual practice and the destruction of American Indian culture. This parallels the earlier destruction of pre-Christian Western European culture.

Allen defines *ritual* as " . . . a procedure whose purpose is to transform someone or something from one condition or state to another."[18] In stating this, Allen agrees with Turner that the intent of ritual is change or transformation.

It is noteworthy that Allen makes a connection between women-centered cultures and women-centered rituals. It may be no coincidence then that in the process of reclaiming personal and collective power, women are turning or returning to women-centered ritual.

Framework for This Study

The framework for examining ritual in this study was drawn from *The Abingdon Dictionary of Living Religions*. *The Abingdon Dictionary* discusses these elements of ritual:

14

- Identity and transformation in ritual
- The done, the said, and the seen
- The context of ritual: symbolic time and space
- Types of ritual

The following are excerpts from *The Abingdon Dictionary*, which explain the above elements of ritual.

Identity and Transformation

Abingdon discusses how ritual affirms "the participants' identity at the same time that it makes transformation of that identity possible."[19] Social, psychological, and historical identities and transformation are examined further:

Social identity. Rituals often serve to put the participants in touch with their social context, to enable them to affirm that they are a part of a particular community or clan, as if by means of socio-drama they can work out the conflicts that their various social alliances may imply.[20]

Psychological and intellectual identity. Ritual also affords identity of a psychological and intellectual kind insofar as it can make the participant aware of values, beliefs, and needs, as well as tensions with the larger social and political order.[21]

Historical identity. Another less noticed way in which ritual affirms one's identity is in its evocation of "history." Myths which describe how the ritual or the sacred community—or even the world itself—began are often recited during the ritual.[22]

15

Transformation. Yet there is a paradox in the ritual process. Beyond the affirmation of an established identity, ritual may "transform" the participant and provide a new identity.[23]

The Done, the Said, and the Seen

The symbols and language of ritual speak on many different levels and through many media, and engage and appeal to all the senses . . . Yet ritual symbolism has been most commonly examined and interpreted in terms of three components; what is done, what is said, and what is seen.[24]

What is done. One part of the symbolic intent of ritual is expressed in a sequence of performed acts. These acts taken together often constitute a process which implies transition from one stage of being to another. From this perspective, ritual is designed to reflect the process of growth and maturation whether it is of a social order, of culture, or of religious awareness.[25]

What is said. Utterances during the ritual process can be doxological propositions of faith . . . or of sonority which enhances awareness of the numinous, the utterance of sounds, chants, mantras, or prayers, and the recitation of myths or sacred history which tell participants how and why things are as they are.[26]

What is seen. The visible paraphernalia of ritual convey their own meanings which reinforce and supplement the symbolism of action and sound. The visual symbols used in ritual include color, numbers, shapes, animals, vessels, vestments, food stuffs, and hosts of other combinations.[27]

The Context of Ritual: Symbolic Time and Space

Ritual space. Certain places take on specific importance in the ritual experience [such as cities—Mecca, Jerusalem, etc., or buildings—temples, churches]. In addition to traditional ritual spaces any number of places can be ritually sacralized (a house, a cavern, a riverbank, the foot of a tree, a hilltop) and these become meaningful contexts for ritual events.[28]

Ritual time. When specific movements of chronological measured time open into the sacred realm beyond time, they become tempocosms or occasions for ritual beginnings, maturations, or breakthroughs. The solar year with its new year and equinoxes, the lunar cycles, the agricultural year with its seasons of planting, monsoon, and harvest, etc.[29]

Types of Ritual

Corporate, domestic, personal rituals. A corporate ritual is one which is community based and serves as a means of creating or affirming the community at large. In domestic ritual the home (or a sacralized place in it) is understood to be sacred cosmos and the parent (or a private functionary) becomes the ritual technician. Personal rituals are done in solitude or at least without a structured social context. Such rituals tend to be in places and times that have meaning in one's personal history and express the identity and needs of the person or individual.[30]

Rituals of healing. Rituals designed to bring about wholeness in the human and cosmic realms represent yet another type. They are specifically intended to restore health or purity and exercise evil influences from body, mind, or place.[31]

Festivals. Festivals are celebrated in virtually every society at appropriate junctures of the year in such a way as to make those junctures meaningful. One might make a distinction between two kinds of festival—the ecofest and the theofest. An ecofest is a festival which celebrates an astronomical or seasonal event to make it an occasion for remembrance, renewal, or breakthrough to the cosmic significance of that event. A theofest is a festival primarily designed to celebrate some event in the life of a deity or sacred being.[32]

Rites of passage. These rituals are designed to enhance the significance and psychic safety of periods of change in one's lifetime [e.g., birth, entrance to adulthood, death, funerals, etc.]. In one sense, virtually all ritual can be characterized as rites of passage insofar as it permits social and personal passage from one mode of being to another.[33]

Framework Summary

The Abingdon Dictionary describes four elements of ritual: identity and transformation; the done, the said, and the seen; the context of ritual—symbolic time and space; and types of ritual. These elements were drawn upon in designing this study.

Literature Summary

All of the preceding books, essays, and journals have been influential in shaping the course and the form of women's ritual. The works of Merlin Stone, Margaret Murray, and Matilda Joslyn Gage provide roots and historical background of women's roles in prepatriarchal cultures. In particular, they explore women's roles in the religious or spiritual practices of these societies. They also recover strong female images or symbols in the form of "goddesses." Women in ritual are reclaiming these female images as role models to emulate and thereby empower themselves.

In addition to these works related to the roots of women's spirituality, practitioners of women's ritual look to contemporary works that examine women's spirituality. Carol Christ and Judith Plaskow's anthology, *Womanspirit Rising*, contains the writings of several spiritual feminists. These women write about their own personal stories, their research into the roots of women's spirituality, and/or about rituals they have created and performed.

In her essay "Contemporary Feminist Rituals," Kay Turner writes about the need for, and the importance of, women's ritual. In addition, she discusses several key elements of women's ritual. These include creating sacred space, female bonding, self-transformation, societal transformation, and forming a relationship between self and community.

Three authors contributing to the actual form of women's ritual are three Bay Area women, Z. Budapest, Hallie Iglehart, and Starhawk. Their books provide background information, both personal and historical, for guiding women in creating and performing rituals for themselves.

Two new cross-cultural works discussing ritual are *Jambalaya*, by Luisah Teish, and *The Sacred Hoop*, by Paula Gunn Allen. Both of these authors are also Bay Area women. In their books, they discuss their cultures. In both of their traditions, women's role was highly regarded before white patriarchal colonizers destroyed much of their culture. These women are reclaiming their woman-centered cultures, and they write extensively about the importance of ritual in their traditions.

These last two books offer new and broadening perspectives on women's ritual. All of the writers' works reviewed in this chapter have influenced and continue to influence the shape of women's ritual.

Literature on the subject of women's spirituality is very extensive. See the Bibliography for an expanded list of written works pertaining to women's spirituality and/or women's ritual.

CHAPTER III
Research Methods

Subjects

A sample of five ritual groups in the San Francisco Bay Area participated in this study. The sample was drawn by personal contacts. The sample groups were chosen with the intent of representing the diversity in practice of women's spirituality. The groups were informed of the purpose of this study. They were also informed that all the participants in the study would be provided with a summary of the study's results. The sample for this study is not necessarily representative of all women's ritual groups.

Research Methods

The research for this text was conducted in two phases. The first phase was a written questionnaire given to all women in each of the five ritual groups. This amounted to a total of sixty-three questionnaires. Thirty-three of the sixty-three questionnaires were completed and returned to the researcher. The second phase of research was an interview of a subsample of women selected from each of the five groups.

Questionnaire

An original questionnaire was constructed to elicit data needed to respond to the guiding research questions. A draft of the questionnaire was pilot-tested with a knowledgeable respondent who was not part of a ritual group. Questionnaires were sent to group leaders, or other contacts, for distribution to group members during the month of November 1986. The questionnaire requested basic demographic information. There were also general questions regarding each ritual group's history, structure, purpose, and other characteristics. Finally, there were questions regarding the relationship of women's ritual to the women's movement, and questions regarding the probability of growth and continuance of women's ritual. A copy of the questionnaire is displayed in Appendix A.

Interview

The second phase of research was a personal interview conducted with two women from each of the five groups participating in this study. The pool from which interviewees were selected consisted of questionnaire respondents who indicated a willingness to participate in a personal interview. In those groups in which more than two respondents were agreeable to an interview, the researcher selected two women from as diverse backgrounds as possible within each group.

The interview delved more extensively into the characteristics of the groups, the type of rituals, the purpose of women's ritual, and its relationship to the larger women's movement. Finally, the interview asked what continuation, modification, and growth can be expected for women's ritual. A copy of the interview schedule is displayed in Appendix B.

CHAPTER IV

Results and Discussion

This chapter is divided into six sections. The six sections are:

Characteristics of Women in the Ritual Groups
Characteristics of the Ritual Groups
Characteristics of Women's Ritual
Roots and Sources of the Groups' Rituals
Growth Prospects
Relationship to the Women's Movement

Characteristics of Women in the Ritual Groups

In order to learn about the characteristics of women in Bay Area women's ritual groups, a questionnaire was sent to the members of five Bay Area women's ritual groups. Sixty-three questionnaires were sent to the members of the five groups. Thirty-three questionnaires were completed and returned.

The five women's ritual groups participating in this study are all located within a forty-mile radius of San Francisco. The names of the participants and their groups are confidential. For purposes of this study, the groups are referred to as Group A, B, C, D, and E.

Group A is a women's ritual group/class led by two Bay Area women who have been involved with women's ritual for a number of years. Seven members of Group A returned completed questionnaires for this study.

Group B is a women's ritual group with some members identifying themselves as witches and/or as priestesses. Of the five groups studied, this is the only group whose members identified as such. Five members of Group B returned completed questionnaires.

Group C is comprised of women from a non-Judeo-Christian church who have developed their own women's ritual group services outside of their traditional church services. Nine members of Group C returned the questionnaire.

Group D is a women's ritual group. Four members of Group D returned the questionnaire. Three of the four identify their occupations as therapists.

Group E was a women's ritual group. After three years of existence, Group E disbanded in the fall of 1986, a few weeks before the research questionnaire for this study was sent out. Because part of this study asks about probabilities of growth for women's ritual, it was decided this group could offer valuable information on this question. Thus, the group was included. Eight members of Group E returned the questionnaire.

The questionnaire began with questions about the background of the individuals completing the questionnaire. The following is a compilation of the responses to those questions.

Group Demographics

There were no women under the age of twenty or over the age of seventy who completed the questionnaire. There were two women between the ages of twenty and thirty and one woman between the ages of sixty and seventy. This was followed by six women between the ages of fifty and sixty, ten women between the ages of forty and fifty, and the largest number of women, fourteen, between the ages of thirty and forty. The breakdown of ages by group is as follows:

Table 1
Age Distribution of Respondents

Age	20-29	30-39	40-49	50-59	60-69	Group Total
Group A	1	3	1	2		7
Group B		2	1	1	1	5
Group C	1	4	2	2		9
Group D			3	1		4
Group E		5	3			8
Age Totals	2	14	10	6	1	

Groups A, B, and C have the widest range of ages. The range for both Group A and Group C is 20 to 60 years of age, while the range for Group B is 30 to 70 years of age. Using the five groups as an indicator of interest and involvement in women's ritual groups, women aged 30 to 50 are most likely to be interested in and participate in women's ritual.

The ethnic makeup of the five groups is overwhelmingly "white," with twenty-two respondents indicating some form of Euro-American background and ten identifying as Jewish or mixed Jewish-European background. One respondent left this question blank.

A variety of occupations were listed by the respondents. Except for those listing themselves as students, most of the respondents are professionals in some type of service profession. Thirteen respondents identified their occupation as some form of human service profession. Among these, seven are in the mental health profession and four are in alternative health professions. In addition, three identified as teachers and one as a minister. Except for the students, the remainder are in some type of business or business service.

All the respondents have education beyond high school. Ten have a bachelor's degree, and an eleventh will receive her bachelor's degree this spring. Sixteen other respondents have a master's degree and one has a law degree. Another will receive her law degree, J.D., this spring.

The income levels of the respondents range from under $10,000 annually to over $50,000 annually. Among the three respondents who listed their income as under $10,000, two are students. The third is a dance and yoga teacher who is married but listed only her income on the questionnaire. The individual income of most of the respondents is in the $20,000-to-$30,000 range (see table 2).

Table 2
Annual Income of Respondents

Income	Under $10,000	$10,000/ $19,999	$20,000/ $29,999	$30,000/ $39,999	$40,000/ $49,999	$50,000 and over
Group A		2	3	1	1	
Group B		1	2	2		
Group C	2	4	2	1		
Group D		1	1	2		
Group E	1	1	4			2
Income Totals	3	9	12	6	1	2

Twenty-eight respondents indicated the income they

listed is their income alone. The other five respondents indicated the income they listed is their combined family income. No respondent listed her partner's income as her only income. Among the five respondents who listed a combined family income, three are in the $30,000-to-$40,000 income range and two are in the over-$50,000 range.

The marital status of the thirty-three respondents is nine married and twenty-four unmarried. No respondent in Group A is married, and only two of the nine respondents in Group C are married. This is followed by three of the eight respondents in Group E who are married. In Group B, two of the five respondents are married, and in Group D, two of the four respondents are married.

The sexual orientation of the respondents is as follows: twenty-two heterosexual, five lesbian, and four bisexual. Two respondents left this question blank. Two respondents in Group A are lesbian, and one respondent in Group B, C, and E is lesbian. One respondent in Group A and in Group C is bisexual, and two respondents in Group E are bisexual. Group D is the only group in which all respondents identified as heterosexual.

The respondents were asked whether or not they have children. Thirteen respondents have children of their own, one has stepchildren only, and nineteen respondents have no children. Group B is the only group in which all the respondents have children. In Group C, it is almost evenly divided with four of the nine respondents having children. In the other groups, the majority are childless. In Group A, five out of seven have no children; in Group D, three out of four have no children; and in Group E, six out of eight have no children.

Composite Profile

Based on this background information of the respondents in this study, a composite profile of a woman in a Bay Area ritual group can be made. She is white, aged thirty to forty, and has a master's degree. In addition, she is a professional in a human services occupation with an income of $20,000 to $30,000 per year. Finally, she is heterosexual, unmarried, and has no children.

Characteristics of the Ritual Groups

This section examines six characteristics of the women's ritual groups in this study. The six characteristics include: the origins of the group; group membership and rules; when and where the groups' rituals are held; and the group's decision-making processes. In addition, this section asks whether or not the groups are "spiritual" and whether or not they are "religious."

Origins of the Groups

Most of the ritual groups in this study have informal beginnings. Three groups resulted when a group of women just decided to do rituals together. Another group is a women's ritual class, and another originated from a workshop on women's ritual.

Group A was formed as a ritual class in the fall of 1986. There were about fifteen women in this group. The class was continuing in 1987, and most women were expected to continue the class. One of the teachers in this class has been teaching women's ritual in the Bay Area for more than twelve years.

Group B began with a few women who wanted to practice ritual and decided to get together for this purpose. Questionnaire respondents in Group B varied slightly in their response to how long this group has existed. Respondents indicated the group has existed from four to six years. The two respondents who participated in the interview were probed more extensively about the origin of their group. One interviewee from this group was vague about the origins, and the other said she knew nothing about the origins. There are eleven women in this group.

Group C evolved out of a church women's continental spiritual renewal event several years ago. The women felt frustrated after this event and "decided [they] needed to do things at a grassroots level [themselves]." Women at this event from the Northern California area developed an annual weekend event of women's ritual. This group has existed for three years. Approximately 125 women attend the annual women's weekend event. However, the questionnaire for this study was sent only to the twenty women who meet regularly to plan the annual weekend event.

Group D is an offshoot of a more organized women's ritual training workshop. Using methods devised by and learned from this "parent" organization, Group D now functions independently. This group has existed for two years, and there are six to eight women in the group.

Group E evolved out of a "Women in Religion" study group. A small core from the study group met and did a ritual together over three years ago. From that experience their group developed into a women's ritual group. This is the group that disbanded in the fall of 1986. There were eight to twelve women in this group. (Three women from

30

this group have decided to form a new ritual group of their own.)

When asked how they learned about women's ritual, most respondents said they learned through a friend. The length of time the respondents have been doing ritual ranges from as short as ten months to as long as fourteen years. The average length of time for the thirty-three respondents is 5.7 years. However, the actual amount of time listed more than any other is 2 years. Group E is the most experienced group. Respondents from this group listed a range of 6 1/2 to 14 years doing women's ritual. In addition to one respondent in Group E who listed 14 years, two other respondents in this group listed 12 years of doing women's ritual.

Group Membership and Rules

Membership

The two respondents from each group who participated in the interview for this study were asked if their groups have membership requirements. Four groups have some type of membership requirement, and one group has no membership requirements.

Group C is the only group that does not have membership requirements. One interviewee said they had no membership requirements because they are "deliberately not an organization and [they] don't want to create one."

However, none of the other four groups have particularly formalized membership requirements. Most interviewees gave responses such as "a desire to be in the group" and "a commitment to attend ritual meetings." Some groups require prospective members to have studied or practiced women's ritual before joining their group. Two groups, B and E, require group consensus for accepting a new member into their group.

Rules

In general, the five groups have no strictly uniform rules. However, within each group, there is a general understanding of what is expected of the participants.

When asked if their groups have any rules, the interviewees in Group A and Group E said, "No," though both groups indicated there are some basic understandings about the group process among the ritual participants. The rules for Groups B, C, and D are not "codified." In general, the interviewees from these three groups were somewhat vague, and the interviewees within each group did not give the same responses as to what exactly their group's rules are. Some of the rules they listed are:

- "Only members may attend rituals."
- "Those attending a ritual agree to participate in the ritual and to listen when another is speaking."
- "Confidentiality—either about what is said in the ritual or who is attending the ritual."
- "Agree to use group consensus to make group decisions."

The interviewees were asked if visitors are ever allowed to attend their rituals. This question was not applicable to Group C since they have no membership requirements. Among the other four groups, both A and D do not allow visitors to attend rituals, and Groups B and E do allow visitors to attend rituals. However, both Group B and E allow visitors to attend only certain specified rituals.

32

When and Where Are the Rituals?

When

When asked when they meet to perform rituals, each of the five groups varied considerably. Group A, the ritual class, meets weekly for a certain number of weeks and then takes a break. Group B meets at the full moons and new moons and at the Celtic or pagan holidays. (These holidays are summer and winter solstice, on or near June 21 and December 21; spring and fall equinox, on or near March 21 and September 21; Candlemas, February 2; May Eve or Beltane, April 30; Lammas, August 1; and Samhain or Hallowmas, October 31.)

Group C meets annually for one full weekend of rituals. This weekend event is held in the fall. However, a subgroup, which plans this event, meets periodically throughout the year to plan the event and they occasionally do a ritual at these planning meetings. Group D meets every other week for eight weeks. Then they take a break, usually for four weeks. After the break, they return and renew their commitment to another eight weeks of ritual meetings. Group E no longer meets. However, before they disbanded, they met at the full moons and at summer and winter solstice and spring and fall equinox.

Where

Where the groups gather to hold their rituals also varies somewhat. Group A meets in a classroom in an alternative health center in the East Bay. Groups B and E rotate gathering at the various members' homes. On occasion these two groups do rituals outdoors—on a hillside, at a park, or in a member's backyard. Group C holds its

33

annual weekend event at a different campsite in Northern California each year. The site rotates in order to make it available to women in different areas and also to avoid "cliquishness." One interviewee from Group C acknowledged it would make planning a lot easier if they used the same site each year, but they feel their commitment to accessibility to as many as possible supersedes the ease of using the same site each year. Finally, Group D meets regularly at one of the member's home.

Decision-Making Process

There is similarity among some of the groups in their decision-making process. Each group said all their participants have some say in the group's decision-making. Group A has the most limited participant input in that the general structure and content of the class are decided by the teacher. The students, however, are asked for some input, at times, in choosing a theme for the rituals. Group B is also somewhat limiting in participant input. This group has a smaller group of "priestesses," who make some of the group's decisions. One interviewee said they were "more of an oligarchy than a democracy," and she did not know what process the priestesses use to make their decisions. However, Group B makes decisions about when to meet and about who may join their group by consensus.

The interviewees in Group C said all the members of their core planning group participate in making decisions (the core group consists of twenty women who were sent questionnaires for this study). They said they decide by consensus. However, they note there are sometimes long debates before a final consensus decision is reached. Group D is somewhat similar to Group C in that they use a "consensus decision process" to make decisions and "all are satisfied" with the decisions reached. Group E is also similar to the last two groups in their decision-making procedure. They made decisions "collectively through consensus."

Are Women's Ritual Groups Spiritual?

Women's ritual is usually thought of in relation to women's spirituality. In order to determine whether the participants in these groups regard their groups as "spiritual," the interviewees were asked to give their definition of spiritual. Then they were asked whether, based on their definition, they regard their groups as spiritual. The following are the interviewees' definitions of spiritual:

Group A

First interviewee: "It is getting in touch with that part of yourself unconnected to logic or emotion, but a lot of connection to truth and love and the intangible parts of yourself—the psychic, unconscious, intuitive, creative elements, and connected with behavior."
Second interviewee: "The whole. What holds everything together."

Group B

First interviewee: "A form of worship with a central theme of the Goddess within. The power and energy I picture as the all-encompassing Goddess or Mother Nature. Using that to make a difference in the world."
Second interviewee: "A desire to find a context other than

that which we commonly call reality. What's beyond provable or known. For me it is essentialism versus existentialism. Beyond the selfness—breaking limits—the cutting edge."

Group C

First interviewee: "When I can make a connection with my entire being—my intellect, emotions, and physical self."

Second interviewee: "Whatever is going on—listening, watching, singing—what experience is talking to my emotions, not my intellect. An emotional, not intellectual experience. Not wanting to be defined."

Group D

First interviewee: "A part of the self, oriented to the transpersonal self, or those activities or processes that are oriented to the transpersonal self."

Second interviewee: "A witness to higher consciousness to have a transpersonal perspective on daily living. Mystery, awe of the universe. Treating each person as the god or goddess within. A sense of the divine."

Group E

First interviewee: "Viewing our lives in a larger context, beyond the human and the planetary. Being connected to a larger whole beyond the human."

Second interviewee: "A world view. What your values are. It's what religion is. Spiritual may be more of the day to day expression of your religion."

When asked if, based on their definition, their groups are spiritual groups, all ten interviewees said, "Yes." One qualified her response saying, "Yes and no. Sometimes we come from that place."

Summary

The interviewees gave a range of responses in their definition of "spiritual." According to the interviewees, spiritual is connected to an inner part of a person and it is personal. For some, though, it also means connecting them to something outside of themselves, such as connecting them to nature, to other people, or to "the whole." Several said it was not intellectual, but rather intangible or connected to intuitive, creative, and/or emotional parts of themselves. And for some it has to do with moving beyond the physical or personal and "transcending." One interviewee said it does not want to be defined. This may sum up why many of the definitions of spiritual tend to be somewhat abstract.

Several interviewees' definitions of spiritual are similar to the definition of feminist spirituality provided in chapter I. The definition in chapter I states feminist spirituality is "the process of integration, of connection." This corresponds to those interviewees who defined spiritual as a connection within the self and/or with other people, nature, and other external beings, objects, or phenomena. Some interviewees' definitions of spiritual differed from that in chapter I, particularly on the concept of "transcending." For some interviewees, spiritual was defined as "transcending" the self or the physical. However, the definition in chapter I defined feminist spirituality as specifically not focused on transcending the self or everyday life. Rather, feminist spirituality is focused on "recognizing the power in everyday life" and "integrating one's ego-self with the collective self." However they define spiritual, all of the interviewees regard their ritual groups as spiritual.

Are Women's Ritual Groups Religious?

Since the terms "spiritual" and "religious" are often connected with each other, and since ritual in general is frequently thought of in relation to religions, the interviewees were asked whether or not they regard their groups as "religious." However, they were first asked to define "religious." The following are their definitions of religious:

Group A

First interviewee: "It is holding a certain ideology or belief that somehow seems irrefutable. Having a doctrine and belief system. An institution, a practice and set of beliefs. Religion doesn't have to come from inside. It's based on behavior and belief."
Second interviewee: "Someone affiliated with a religion—organized and defined by someone else."

Group B

First interviewee: "An organized church with a minister or priest—usually patriarchal, often Christian. Religion is formal."
Second interviewee: "A commitment to self that involves a deep philosophical inquiry."

Group C

First interviewee: "The root meaning of religion is 'to bind together over and over again.' "

Second interviewee: "Religion is based on the spiritual. It involves more of the intellectual or thinking, talking or writing about. It implies a unified way of doing it. Everybody who belongs to that religion has a unified way of talking about or speaking about it. A whole other experience because they're doing it as a group, not as an individual. Feeling connected to a community versus individual."

Group D

First interviewee: "Its origin means 'to yoke, to be yoked.' "

Second interviewee: "Reverencing the godhead. In the 'New Age,' it means experiencing the God within, not the God without, which is the former definition."

Group E

First interviewee: "An institution with a clearly defined belief in practice. A history with belief in traditions. Having a decision-making power structure. A clearly defined community, organized religion."

Second interviewee: "The same definition as spiritual. A world view of values."

When asked if, based on their definition of religious, they would describe their group as religious, five interviewees said, "No," four said, "Yes," and one said, "Yes and no." In only two groups were both interviewees in agreement on this. In Group B both interviewees said, "No," they

39

would not describe their group as religious. In Group C both interviewees said, "Yes." In the other three groups, the two interviewees were divided on this question.

Summary

The interviewees were somewhat varied in their definitions of "religious." Two interviewees gave root definitions for religious. These were "to bind together over and over" and "to yoke or to be yoked." The others gave their own definitions. For most of the others, religious means an organization or institution with a dogma or set of beliefs, which all who belong must adhere to.

In general, religious is more structured and organized than is spiritual. As one interviewee said, "religious doesn't have to come from inside." In contrast, most interviewees' definitions of spiritual were that it is personal and indeed comes "from inside." Also, "spiritual" almost defies structure while "religious" requires structure. This suggests there is a correlation between viewing "religious" as referring to an external organization and some interviewees saying their ritual group is not religious.

While all interviewees regard their ritual groups as spiritual, five interviewees do not regard their ritual groups as religious. Also, a sixth interviewee is mixed, saying, "Yes and no" when asked if she regards her group as religious. Fewer than half the interviewees regard their ritual groups as religious.

Characteristics of Women's Ritual

Commonalities

There is a wide range of diversity and creativity in what is done both among and within the five groups studied for this text. Yet, a basic format of ritual emerges that is similar for all the rituals described by the interviewees from the five groups.

Three Parts of Ritual

The basic format that emerged includes three parts: The first part is what the interviewees describe as creating "sacred space" for performing the rituals. The second part is the "core" or the "heart" of the ritual. During the core, the transformation work of the ritual is performed. The transformation work is based on a theme or issue that the ritual participants and/or the ritual leaders have chosen for that particular ritual. The third basic part of women's ritual is an ending of the ritual.

Purpose of Part 1: Creating Sacred Space
The interviewees were asked the purpose of or reason the various portions of their rituals are performed. When asked the purpose of creating "sacred space," a frequent response was that they create a sacred space in order for them to have a "safe place" to be together and to be themselves. Another common response was that creating a sacred space takes them out of their everyday time and space and everyday cares or stresses. They are in a special place where outside responsibilities can be put aside and they can focus on the intent of the ritual.

Common experiences during part 1.

When asked what they experienced during this part of the ritual, most of the interviewees indicated feeling a sense of being in a special place. Several also said they experience a sense of "community," "connection," or bonding with the other ritual participants.

Purpose of Part 2: The Core of the Rituals

The purpose of the core phase of the ritual is to do some type of transformation work. Usually this transformation work is to bring about a change for the individual ritual participants, though several interviewees said that sometimes they may choose a theme around ecological, social, or "planetary" issues for their transformative work.

Common experiences during part 2.

A common experience for the interviewees during this phase is a sense of "getting in touch" with themselves. Another common experience is that they feel empowered at this time. They feel like they really can make a change.

Purpose of Part 3: The Ending of the Rituals

The purpose of the ending phase of the ritual is to give the participants a sense of closure. Interviewees also said it is to prepare them to leave their "sacred space," and to prepare them to take their transformed feelings or energy with them as they return to everyday time and space.

Common experiences during part 3.

When asked what they experience during the ending phase of their rituals, most interviewees said they feel a sense of completion and a transition to daily life.

Variations

While there is a basic three-part format common among the five ritual groups studied, there is a wide variety of ways the groups perform these three parts of women's ritual.

Part 1: Creating Sacred Space

All five groups use the form of a circle for their sacred space. The different ways the groups create sacred space include smudging, using the four elements, invoking or calling the four directions, singing, chanting, wordless chanting or sounding, meditation, and visualization. Smudging is burning sage and using the smoke of the burning sage to cleanse or purify the participants and/or the ritual space.

The four elements are earth, air, fire, and water. Each element or a symbol of the element (such as a feather to symbolize air, or salt to symbolize earth) is passed over the circle and/or around the ritual participants to "consecrate" and/or "purify" the space and the participants. As the element is passed around, something is usually said about what that element symbolizes. For example, fire might symbolize or represent light, warmth, or energy, including sexual energy.

Another method for creating sacred space is "invoking" the four directions. To do this, one or several ritual participants face east, south, west, and north. When facing each direction, the ritual participant asks that direction and the power or energy that direction represents or symbolizes to be with the group. For example, in this hemisphere, north is usually affiliated with the element earth and represents the powers of the earth, of stability, darkness, mountains, caves, and animals who live in caves or climb mountains. The four directions are also sometimes connected with various heroines or goddesses who symbolize the power a particular direction represents. For example, the Hawaiian Goddess Pele is associated with the element fire, which is associated with the direction south. Pele represents the power of fire and the power of volcanoes. When invoking the four directions then, a goddess may be named, or called, for the particular power or energy she symbolizes.

The interviewees gave similar reasons for using the elements and for invoking the four directions, in creating sacred space. The reasons for using the elements and invoking the directions include: "to help [them] get out of [their] heads and get in touch with the physical or natural world"; to "connect with the earth and remember [themselves] as part of the natural world"; and to "step into another space."

Another way of creating sacred space is to have the ritual participants physically create it by first forming a line outside the circle and then, either in silence or singing, entering the circle. The ritual participants usually form the line and enter the circle in some order. The order is most often chronological, i.e., oldest to youngest or vice versa. However, one group said they have also formed their line of entry to the circle based on their calendar year birthdays, i.e., those with January birthdays enter first followed by those with birthdays in each of the following months.

All five groups use one or a combination of the preceding methods to begin the process of creating sacred space.

Following this, the groups continue creating sacred space by using one or more of the following methods to help focus or center the ritual participants. These methods include singing, chanting, wordless chanting or sounding, meditation, or visualization. This is done to continue creating sacred space and to help the participants focus on the "intent" of the ritual.

Various Experiences While Creating Sacred Space

When asked what they experience while creating sacred space, interviewees listed a variety of experiences in addition to the common experience of feeling a sense of connection or community with the other ritual participants. Among the experiences reported are: "releasing pent-up emotions or tensions"; "closing the space to the outside world"; feeling "the body more clearly"; feeling "calmer"; "given permission to be [her] womanself"; "focusing inward"; and feeling "physically connected."

In addition to these inner feelings and experiences, some interviewees also note outer experiences, such as feeling "integrated with a larger reality" and feeling "energized with both personal and divine power." Finally, one interviewee is very moved when doing sounding (sounding is using the voice to make wordless sounds). In her experience with sounding, she said she feels "like women have been making these sounds since the beginning of time and we are picking it up and carrying it along."

Part 2: The Core of the Ritual

Once the "sacred space" is created and the participants are centered or focused, the core or heart of the ritual begins. Here the widest variety of activity and creativity, both within and among the groups, is reported. There is always a ritual theme, and what is done during the core reflects that theme. Most frequently interviewees report a theme that is focused on themselves—a theme to gain insight into themselves and/or to change themselves.

According to the interviewees, there are many ways in which this core work is done. Among the ways reported are re-enacting or reciting woman-centered mythologies, stories, plays, poetry, or other readings; focusing on a ritual object while being led in a visualization and imagining how that object is transformed; clay sculpting; sharing dreams or spiritual experiences; mask making; dancing or movement; drawing pictures; doing massage or bodywork; doing other healing work; teaching; discussing and sharing experiences based on the theme; inner journeying or trancework; reading Tarot cards or Rune stones; and/or singing.

In addition, Group C, the largest group, creates a smaller circle of approximately twenty women during the core of their rituals. A small group of women is asked to come to the center to form a smaller circle. These women are asked to share their experiences or insights, based on the theme. Those in the inner circle may share by talking, singing, dancing or movement, silence, or whatever works best for the individual. Ritual participants rotate being in the small inner circle throughout the weekend of rituals in order that all who attend are in the center circle and share at least once during the weekend.

Additional Core Themes

Groups B and E report they observe winter and summer solstices, and spring and fall equinoxes. Their core theme is then focused on the meaning or symbolism of the particular solstice or equinox being observed. For instance, spring equinox might have a theme of new beginnings, new growth, or renewal.

In addition to the aforementioned holidays, Group B also observes four other Celtic or pagan holidays. These are Candlemas, Beltane or May Eve, Lammas, and Hallowmas. Again, the core themes for these rituals revolve around the symbolism for these holidays. Candlemas symbolizes purification and initiation; Beltane symbolizes the fruits of spring, fertility, and sexuality; Lammas symbolizes the harvest and abundance; and Hallowmas symbolizes the end and the beginning, death and rebirth or regeneration, and it is a time to honor the dead.

Interviewees also indicate that sometimes the theme for the core is based on social, ecological, or planetary issues. These include women's issues, peace issues, and healing the earth. However, as stated previously, the core work is most often based on a personal theme for the participants' own change or self-transformation.

Various Experiences during the Core

Besides feeling in touch with themselves and feeling empowered during the core of the ritual, interviewees also list the following experiences:

- "letting go of the past and a door opening to new possibilities"
- "a new life"
- "happy, energetic, and renewed"
- "a range—from feeling nothing to gaining new insights"
- "boredom"
- "feeling [her] body throbbing"
- "feeling safe and able to take risk"
- "feeling a connection to the others [at the ritual]"
- "a sense of adventure"
- "a transcending experience"
- "some sense of hesitancy a times—whether to risk sharing"
- "a sense of awe and wonder at the beauty and depth of those sharing"
- "feeling enriched"

- "feeling supported, reassured, and amazed"
- "thankfulness for sisterhood"
- "feeling okay to talk about the dark side [of herself] and then feeling transformed"
- "feeling more physically whole"
- "feeling greater energy and greater hope"
- "feeling in touch with the unseen and the underground—making it real"
- "feeling power, love, and clarity being generated"
- "senses a much more fluid consciousness"

These experiences suggest that as a result of women's ritual, the participants do feel transformed and empowered. They also indicate participants experience being in a safe place and feel a connection with each other.

Part 3: The Ending

Like the first two parts of women's ritual, the third part, the ending, is also done in a variety of ways. These include grounding the participants; releasing the four directions by thanking them for their energy and/or saying good-bye to them; holding hands and singing; going around the circle and having each participant say a short word or phrase regarding how they feel or what they got out of the ritual; singing; giving thanks for what they received at the ritual; chanting; and/or dancing.

Various Experiences during the Ending
At the ending the interviewees indicate a number of experiences including: feeling "grateful"; feeling "a cohesiveness"; feeling "nothing"; "pulling all the emotions in and putting them inside as [they] prepare to go back into the other world"; "a sense of what [she] got out of the

ritual"; "enjoyment of the shared activity"; "fulfillment, completion, elation, sisterhood, splendor, and satiation."

As ritual participants end their ritual then, they experience gratitude, fulfillment, and a sense of community. They also prepare to return to their everyday lives.

Other Activities Included in Some Rituals

In addition to the previously mentioned activities, some of the groups also create an altar on which ritual or symbolic objects are placed. Among the objects that might be placed on the altar are candles, pictures, flowers, incense, rocks, sea shells, the elements, and crystals. In some groups the altar is placed in the center of their circle (on the floor or on a small table), and it is laid out or prepared either just before the ritual or during the "creating space" phase. These groups then form their circle around the altar.

Also, some groups said they "feast" or share food at their rituals. This is done either just before the end of the ritual or right after the end of the ritual.

Finally, some groups reported they do ritual business, such as scheduling a time and choosing a theme for the next ritual, either during or right after the ritual. For those groups who do business during their rituals, the business is done either during the core or else during the food-sharing phase of the ritual.

Summary of Characteristics of Women's Ritual

Women's ritual consists of three basic parts or processes. At the beginning of women's ritual, a "sacred space" is created in which women can let go of everyday cares and become focused on the ritual. Within this sacred space,

49

they feel safe to be themselves. They also feel a bonding or connection with the other women at this time. This last experience of "female bonding" is one of the very significant benefits of women's ritual (see chapter II).

During the second part, the core of women's ritual, the work of the ritual is done. This work is based on a theme. Usually the theme has to do with some type of self-transformation or self-change. At other times, the theme may have to do with societal change. During this phase of the ritual, interviewees report feeling empowered. They also feel like they can change or they can make a difference in their own lives or in the world. This "self-transformation" and the "commitment to . . . transforming society"[1] are among the most important benefits of and reasons for women's ritual (see chapter II).

The final phase of women's ritual is the ending. At this time participants feel a sense of closeness and completion as they prepare to return to their daily lives.

While all five ritual groups report these three basic processes or parts of their rituals, each group varies in the way they perform each process. The core or heart of the ritual is performed with greatest variation both within each group and among the five groups.

Roots and Sources of the Groups' Rituals

In order to determine the roots or sources of their rituals, the interviewees were asked on what traditions, if any, their groups based their rituals. There is some commonality among the five groups regarding the traditions they use. No group follows one tradition only, and all seem quite loose in adapting the traditions they do draw on.

Traditions Used to Create Rituals

The largest influence for Group A's rituals is the "European Neo-Pagan tradition." However, the group also draws heavily on Tibetan Buddhist, Native American, Polynesian, and "any other tradition [they] may come into contact with."

Group B bases their rituals on the "Pagan Sabbats" and "Celtic Faerie, European Witchcraft" tradition. Sometimes they bring in Native American, Egyptian, East Indian, or other traditions.

According to the interviewees in Group C, they "draw upon the world's religions" for their rituals. Among these, they list Wicca, Native American, Jewish, Christian, and Buddhist religions. From these they choose what to use depending on what has meaning to them.

The interviewees in Group D stated they use several traditions including Wicca, Shamanism, Navaho, and other Native American traditions, Judaism, medieval chant, Goddess worship, "Jung's use of the active imagination," art therapy, and yoga.

Group E described their tradition as "eclectic." They based their rituals on Western Goddess/Pagan traditions, Native American spirituality, and the Womanspirit tradition.

Other Sources Used to Create Rituals

All five groups said their rituals are also based on sources other than these traditions. Among the other sources for their rituals are their own creativity, adapting old traditions into ways that are meaningful to the ritual participants, and the feminist movement.

Overall, the interviewees were not specific as to what, in particular, they do in their rituals that directly relates to one tradition or another. The rituals of all five groups reflect the influences of spiritual feminist writers. (See chapter II for a discussion of the published works of some of these spiritual feminists who are influencing the course of women's rituals.) Another large influence on the rituals of the five groups is their own creativity in developing the rituals. In this way, the rituals are able to speak directly to the participants and to their own personal life experiences.

Summary of Roots and Sources of Ritual

In general, the five groups utilize many resources in creating their rituals. They adapt spiritual traditions from many cultures, they use the writings of spiritual feminists, and they draw on their own creativity to design and perform rituals. Probably the most important consideration in designing their rituals is that the ritual meets the needs of the ritual participants.

Growth Prospects

In order to determine whether women's ritual is a growing phenomenon, both the questionnaire and the interview schedule included questions regarding the growth prospects for women's ritual.

Questionnaire Respondents on Growth Prospects

Among the questions asked of the respondents were

how long would they personally continue women's ritual, did they see women's ritual as a growing phenomenon, and what changes did they foresee in women's ritual.

When asked how long they would continue in women's ritual, the overwhelming majority of respondents (twenty) stated always or for the rest of their lives. The remaining thirteen respondents gave answers such as "indefinitely," "don't know," or "for as long as it meets my needs."

The respondents were also asked whether or not they see women's ritual as a growing phenomenon. All thirty-three respondents replied, "Yes." A variety of responses were given when asked why they think it is a growing phenomenon. Among those responses were:

- "It fills a need for spirituality for women that is not available elsewhere."
- "It gives me a chance to stretch myself and feel a oneness with other women."
- "More women I mention it to are interested in groups."
- "Women's awareness of the ways patriarchal religion doesn't satisfy them, as well as the increasing spread of alternative options."

Then the respondents were asked what changes they see for women's ritual as it grows. Their answers included:

- "Small groups coming together to meet and share."
- "It will become more inclusive and diverse."
- "Women from many traditions, including Christian, Jewish, Buddhist, developing feminist rituals."
- "It will become increasingly focused on planetary issues."
- "It will increasingly deal with resolving conflict—personal and beyond."

- "It will be more open. We will be freer to express ourselves and offer it to others without as much fear of censorship."

The questionnaire respondents all agree that women's ritual is growing. They say it is growing because organized religions are not meeting women's spiritual needs, because it gives women an opportunity to grow personally and to bond with other women, and because more and more women are becoming interested in women's ritual.

As women's ritual grows, many respondents foresee changes. The changes they predict are that it will reach more women including those in organized religions and it will become more diverse. In addition, women's ritual groups will broaden their scope to include resolution, from the personal to the global levels. Finally, women's ritual will be more open and available to women in the community and small ritual groups will meet with each other to share information.

Interviewees on Growth Prospects

The two respondents from each group who participated in the interview were probed further about the growth prospects for women's ritual. Among the questions asked were whether they think their group is getting stronger, weaker, or staying the same and whether their group size is increasing, decreasing, or staying about the same.

When asked if they thought their group is getting stronger, weaker, or staying about the same, both interviewees in Groups A, C, and D said, "Stronger." One in Group B said, "Stronger," and one said it "varies": sometimes it feels like it is getting stronger; at other times it feels like it is getting weaker. This question was not applicable to Group E since that group has dissolved.

The interviewees were then asked if their group size is increasing, decreasing, or staying about the same. (This question was not applicable to Group E.) In general, the groups are remaining about the same size, but occasionally gain or lose one or two people. Some interviewees added that they intentionally keep their group a certain size because they don't want the group to get too big. The only group that is growing considerably is Group C. When they held their first weekend ritual three years ago, they had approximately 100 participants. At their Fall 1986 weekend ritual event, they had over 125 participants and they had to turn some people away due to an inability to handle the large number wanting to participate.

Will Women's Ritual Grow?

The interviewees were asked if they thought the women's ritual group movement will grow or stay the same. All ten interviewees said they think it will grow. When asked why they think it will grow, they gave the following responses:

Group A

First interviewee: "It's a mistake to think it's just a women's movement. Rather it's a people's movement that is growing."

Second interviewee: "It's growing from just women to more men and children. We're creating culture within a conducive environment. It will be taught to the rest of the culture."

55

Group B

First interviewee: "I think it'll grow because I'm meeting more and more women interested in joining or forming their own groups. As more learn positively of the group, it will be accepted."

Second interviewee: "Because it's a general movement. I've watched it the last seven to ten years, the New Age type stuff. There is a movement among women who find other vehicles unacceptable, using a lot of male energy and masculine pronouns."

Group C

First interviewee: "Because it's filling a need. The cutting edge of the women's movement is the women's spiritual movement."

Second interviewee: "Because if I assume the women I've met so far are representative, then I think a lot of women are out there with the same kind of needs and feel dissatisfied with traditional organized religion or think that their religion could be enhanced by having women's ritual added."

Group D

First interviewee: "Because we're in a phase where women's increasing consciousness is increasing awareness of feminist values in the religious and the spiritual. The women's movement has gone from economics and politics to the spiritual."

Second interviewee: "It has to grow, there's too much momentum."

Group E

First interviewee: "Because of a deep hunger for women to express spirituality the way they self-define, and not be dominated by men's definition. I find more are starting to do ritual with men though most are comfortable with women-only ritual."

Second interviewee: "I know so many women who are interested in it and who are trying to find a group. I think CR (consciousness raising) left women with an appetite for women's groups."

The interviewees think there are many reasons women's ritual will grow. Some see it as an evolution of the women's movement from the political to the spiritual. Others see so much momentum and interest in women's ritual that it has to grow. Another says women learned from consciousness-raising groups the value of being in women's groups and women's ritual groups meet this need. Also very important is women's need for female imagery and to define themselves spiritually rather than being "dominated by men's definitions." Organized religion is not meeting women's needs. Finally, some see it as not only growing among women but growing to include men and children and to become more of a part of mainstream culture.

Problems or Reasons Women's Ritual May Not Grow

The interviewees were asked if they think there are any problems or reasons why women's ritual groups may not grow. The interviewees replied as follows:

Group A

First interviewee: "It will grow into a community with men. It will be a people's movement."

Second interviewee: "Women's lack of confidence is a big reason. Also, negative competition among women and being too focused on the emotional rather than on what needs to be done."

Group B

First interviewee: "Only public problems, if too many put pressure on people who want to belong. Too many people afraid of the words instead of what is happening. Outsiders' fears. People ostracized for belonging."

Second interviewee: "It's not enough to have a monotheistic system; you need other things to balance the exclusive femaleness. If you believe in the female principle, then you've got to deal with the male. Dealing with the male is missing. Also, it could be it may get so big that the culture may oppress it. There may be a culture backlash."

Group C

First interviewee: "I can't imagine it not growing. It's a brush fire burning out of control. There are elements that would like to control it. A lot of patriarchal church leaders would like to control it, but it's too late."

Second interviewee: "Resistance by some men and women. Male leadership might connect it with witches and heretics. Some resistance to the concept of women daring to have ritual without men."

Group D

First interviewee: "The countervailing forces, the whole dominance of patriarchal culture and women encultured in it. For women themselves, afraid of deviance from social values. They're not given permission to deviate. Also, inherent problems in women's gathering, such as not recognizing and resolving psychological problems inherent in any process whereby women attempt to bond."

Second interviewee: "It may not grow because women in the world are so busy succeeding that there is no time for it."

Group E

First interviewee: "A problem in that all are not able to deal with disagreements and conflicts. This can lead to destructive power dynamics. Also, some women are ready to be with men as well as women. It may be some women will be choosing mixed groups."

Second interviewee: "Lack of knowledge. For some parts of the country, it's too strange. A fear of right-wing backlash."

The most frequent reason given why women's ritual may not grow is because of outside forces or pressures. Many interviewees believe women's ritual may be perceived as a threat to some outsiders who may try to suppress it, or there might be a cultural backlash. Others see problems such as people's lack of knowledge or understanding about women's ritual. Another problem is women's own pressures or stresses in their lives and not having the time to devote to women's ritual.

Some interviewees see internal problems for women's ritual groups. Among these are too much focus on the emotional and not enough on the practical work that needs to be done to keep the groups going. A major internal problem is dealing with interpersonal conflicts within the groups themselves. None of the groups interviewed have an established method for dealing with conflict, and many interviewees perceive this as a problem. Those in Group E said this is the major reason their group dissolved. There were interpersonal problems in their group, and they had no successful method to handle these problems. Women's ritual groups have both external and internal problems that may prevent or slow the growth of the women's ritual movement.

Why Do Some Groups Discontinue?

In connection with problems for women's ritual groups, the interviewees were asked why they think some groups fail to continue. They gave the following answers:

Group A

First interviewee: "People lose interest in getting together and performing the same rituals. There are a lot of choices in the community, and people switch from one group to another group."

Second interviewee: "Lack of commitment is a main one. Also, lack of support in this culture. People need to just take care of themselves because of economic and stress pressures."

Group B

First interviewee: "Group politics. Too many people having problems with those in charge and not enough responsibilities delegated."

Second interviewee: "Around the issues of hierarchy—how to handle it. Groups seem to need someone to give cohesiveness, to pull it together, and the need of people inside to not have an authority figure telling them what to do. Also, interpersonal conflicts. Lack of process or space for processing problems."

Group C

First interviewee: "Some of the creative people are the most overstretched and need to acknowledge having to pay a staff to have the underpinnings taken care of."

Second interviewee: "Some groups get bogged down by individual personalities or conflicts that pull energy away from the group. Or possibly a group is dependent on one small group carrying the group on and falls apart if the leader leaves. There's a danger if the group is dependent on a few leaders or individuals."

Group D

First interviewee: "Not enough time. Multiple demands on women is a given reason, but underneath is their fear of closeness. Also, women's own non-assertiveness and dropping out rather than confronting when needs are not met."

Second interviewee: "Because San Francisco is a transient city. Also, it's hard work and you only have so much time."

Group E

First interviewee: "Not dealing with disagreements and personality conflicts. Also, not willing to risk intimacy."

Second interviewee: "A lot of interpersonal problems are not resolved. Also, some end naturally. They are fulfilled and no longer need the group. Another reason is other commitments and people move away."

One of the main reasons women's ritual groups fail to continue is an inability to resolve conflicts within the groups. There are interpersonal conflicts, and there are conflicts with the power structure. Lack of an effective process to resolve these conflicts leads to an end to some groups. Another major reason women's ritual groups end is a lack of commitment of the participants. Outside demands may supersede commitment to the group, and this weakens the group. Also, some interviewees indicate that an unwillingness to risk intimacy or closeness may result in some groups ending.

How Many Women's Ritual Groups in the Bay Area?

To help assess the popularity and number of women's ritual groups, the interviewees were asked how many other women's ritual groups in the Bay Area they are aware of. The following are their responses:

Group A

First interviewee: "Two or three."

Second interviewee: "I think there are a whole lot I don't know about, but personally I know of about five to ten groups."

Group B

First interviewee: "Approximately thirteen groups."
Second interviewee: "Seven."

Group C

First interviewee: "I think there are probably hundreds, but I couldn't prove it. If I think about it, I could come up with maybe fifteen to twenty-five groups."
Second interviewee: "Maybe one or two I've heard of."

Group D

First interviewee: "Approximately three or four."
Second interviewee: "Three, I'm in or part of three groups."

Group E

First interviewee: "I'd guess there may be one hundred groups."
Second interviewee: "Four."

The number of women's ritual groups the interviewees know of range from just a few to possibly hundreds. This makes it difficult to estimate the number of women's ritual groups existing in the San Francisco Bay Area. It also indicates the lack of publicity existing about women's ritual groups, which may be deliberate on the part of the groups. However, it seems safe to assume there may well be up to one hundred or more women's ritual groups in the Bay Area.

Summary

All respondents in this study agree that women's ritual is a growing movement. They see it growing because there is a lot of interest in it and because it meets needs for women that organized religions do not meet. Also, some see it as an evolution of the women's movement, from the political to the spiritual. Finally, some see it growing to include men and children, and becoming part of mainstream culture.

One of the main problems for women's ritual as it grows is outside pressure by some who may want to suppress it. Other problems are internal problems, especially interpersonal conflicts and participants' lack of commitment.

Despite the problems women's ritual groups must deal with, the respondents in this study are optimistic that this movement will continue to grow.

Relationship to the Women's Movement

In trying to determine whether there is a connection between women's ritual groups and the women's movement, the questionnaire asked respondents whether they consider themselves feminist. It also asked what other women's organizations the respondents are affiliated with.

Respondents' Answers

When asked if they consider themselves feminists, thirty respondents said, "Yes," and three respondents said, "No."

The respondents were then asked what other women's organizations they belong to. Six respondents belong to the National Organization for Women (NOW); three belong to the Women's International League for Peace and Freedom (WILPF); two belong to the Feminist Writers Guild; one belongs to the National Women's Political Caucus (NWPC); and one belongs to the American Association of University Women (AAUW). Eleven respondents also listed other types of women's spirituality groups they belong to in addition to their women's ritual group. Fifteen of the thirty-three respondents did not list any women's organizations they currently belong to.

Interviewees' Expanded Answers

To further explore the relationship of women's ritual groups to the women's movement, the interviewees were asked questions expanding on the previous two questions. First, the interviewees were asked to give their definition of "feminist." These are their definitions:

Group A

First interviewee: "I think of myself as a humanist, not a feminist. Feminist elevates the whole aspect of the feminine, championing the rights of women. Feminism is very dogmatic and rigid."

Second interviewee: "I'm not sure about some of the current contexts of feminism. I'm a feminist spiritually. Change needs to happen on both the material and spiritual realm. Change can't happen on either realm without the other. Real change happens on all levels."

Group B

First interviewee: "A woman who believes in women's rights and the rights of women to be who they are, the freedom to express it. It's more than equality. Everybody should have the right to do what they want to do, with qualifications."

Second interviewee: "A feminist is a female person who wants to change the relationship between people with respect to gender roles and expectations."

Group C

First interviewee: "The word is so loaded I'm almost tired of using it. I prefer 'womanist.' A feminist is feisty, someone who is comfortable in her woman's body and is eager to explore the full capacities of womanhood. A feminist is anti-patriarchal, therefore egalitarian."

Second interviewee: "As a feminist, I do not believe the labels feminine and masculine are a valid way of defining anything. I consider myself a humanist and those values come into play in being a feminist. Judge people as individuals and don't use class and stereotypical categories."

Group D

First interviewee: "Someone who is aware of the bias in values and power that exists in our society against the feminine and who wants to do or is committed to doing something about that."

Second interviewee: "I don't have the language for it. It needs a political vocabulary. Probably a woman think-

ing well of herself. To help women develop themselves."

Group E

First interviewee: "It means women and all humans have the
right to define themselves. The opportunities to develop themselves as they choose to develop. For me
it's tied in to an honoring of the body and the earth.
Both give life and nurture."
Second interviewee: "Someone who doesn't look at the
world through male-oriented eyes. It is equality politically and economically. Opportunities for women. One
who supports women's issues."

The interviewees were then asked if, according to their
definition, they consider themselves feminist. Nine of the
ten interviewees said, "Yes." One said, "No."

In general, the interviewees' definitions of feminist
indicate it means someone who believes in equality for
women and wants to see change made that promotes this
equality. Some expanded the definition to include the right
of people to be who they are and to choose whatever roles
they want regardless of gender.

However, a couple of interviewees had negative responses to the word "feminist." One referred to it as "dogmatic and rigid," and one expressed the need for a new
word because she felt feminist is a "loaded word."

Overall, the majority of interviewees gave positive
definitions of a feminist. In addition, thirty of the thirty-
three questionnaire respondents identify as feminists.

The interviewees were then asked if they were ever
socially or politically active in any aspects of the women's
movement. Eight of the ten interviewees replied, "Yes."

These eight were asked what groups or causes they participated in or in what ways were they active. The eight listed a variety of ways they were active. Among the groups and causes listed are:

- The women's health movement
- Women's spirituality, "which is a maturation of the women's movement"
- NOW
- Working for the ERA
- Pro-choice marcher
- Sending checks to women's rights organizations
- Writing letters to legislators
- Boycotting
- Campus women's groups
- Workshops for women
- "It was my main life form—my career path"
- League of Women Voters
- NWPC
- Women's political funding groups
- AAUW
- Helped open the Women's Building in San Francisco
- Women's Studies Collective
- Organized and facilitated CR groups
- Helped conceive and organize the Great Goddess Conference in Santa Cruz in 1978.
- Battered women's shelters
- Rallied for women's rights

All of the eight were active in at least two or three organizations or causes, and some were active in up to seven or eight organizations or causes.

When asked if they are still active, six of the eight said they are still active. However, most are somewhat less involved than they had been in the past. Some indicated that rather than being actively involved, they prefer to send money to causes they support.

Summary

Six of the ten interviewees are currently involved in the women's movement, and eighteen of the thirty-three respondents currently belong to one or more women's organizations. In addition, thirty of the thirty-three respondents identify as feminists. Finally, eight of the ten interviewees have at one time been active in the women's movement. This suggests that for over half of the participants in this study, there is some connection between the women's movement and women's spirituality. This connection is also supported by the fact that several feminist journals and magazines have featured women's spirituality in one or more of their issues (see chapter II).

Some interviewees expressly stated they think that women's spirituality and women's ritual are an evolution or maturation of the women's movement. Also, some interviewees indicate they now prefer to put their energy into their women's ritual groups rather than into the political and social organizations they were once active in. This suggests there is not only a connection to the women's movement, but that also there may be a trend among some activists to move from mainstream political activism to spiritual activism.

CHAPTER V
Conclusion

This chapter consists of two parts. The first part is an examination of how the ritual framework, used to design this study, applies to women's ritual. The second part is a summary of this study.

The Ritual Framework and Women's Ritual

The framework for studying women's ritual was drawn from *The Abingdon Dictionary of Living Religions* (see chapter II). *The Abingdon Dictionary* discusses four elements of ritual. These elements are:

- Identity and transformation in ritual
- The done, the said, and the seen
- The context of ritual: symbolic time and space
- Types of ritual

The following is an analysis of how these elements of ritual apply to women's ritual.

Identity and Transformation in Ritual

In this element of ritual, *The Abingdon Dictionary* discusses three types of identity: social identity, psychologi-

70

cal identity, and historical identity. It then discusses transformation in ritual. These identities and transformations, as they relate to women's ritual, are discussed below.

Social Identity

Women's ritual begins with women being disconnected from each other in their daily lives. Each goes about her daily life in her various roles—professional, student, employee, etc. When she comes to the ritual, these other identities become much less significant. What is significant is her gender. During women's ritual, a safe place, a "sacred space," is created where it is safe for her to be a woman, with all that that means, including having a woman's body and being a woman in a patriarchal society. In women's ritual, her gender identity becomes her social identity.

Psychological Identity

One of the repeated experiences participants report in women's ritual is the experience of "getting in touch with [themselves]" and "gaining new insights." In women's ritual, participants take risks in sharing some parts of themselves, particularly what some call their "shadow" side, i.e., parts of themselves they may label "bad." In talking about her shadow side during ritual, one interviewee said, "The shadow side became transformed into the positive."

Women use ritual to work through many issues in their lives. These issues include the loss or death of a loved one, recovering from the effects of childhood abuse, learning to love and accept themselves—including their bodies and their sexuality. Ritual is also used to address larger social issues, which may have personal and psychological implications, such as women's issues, ecological issues, and peace issues.

Historical Identity

Participation in women's ritual gives participants a sense of historical identity. Anthropologists are now acknowledging women's powerful roles in prepatriarchal cultures. In ritual, the names of women and goddesses from prepatriarchal cultures are referenced in order that women may emulate these powerful role models. In addition, as feminists reclaim women's history, the heroines and ancestors in women's history are also named in ritual. In this way women can feel a connection with the past and know that there have always been strong women who have had influences in the world.

Transformation

Kay Turner writes that one of the most important things that happens in women's ritual is "self-transformation" (see chapter II). Ritual has the ability to bring about a change in the participants. Ritual participants leave their daily lives behind as they come to the ritual and create a special place, a "sacred space." Once in this sacred space, women feel safe to take risks—to examine and explore themselves and share new insights they have gained.

By participating in the ritual, by taking risks, and by sharing, the participants feel they can change themselves and make changes in their lives. Ritual participants report feeling energized, empowered, and like they have "a new life" after participating in ritual. This ability to bring about transformation is a major reason women participate in women's ritual groups.

The Done, the Said, and the Seen

What Is Done

According to *The Abingdon Dictionary*, ritual consists of "a sequence of performed acts." The purpose of these acts is to offer ritual participants a "transition from one stage of being to another." This ties in closely with the three parts of women's ritual identified in this study.

The participants begin the ritual by making a transition from their everyday life to the sacred space of the ritual. Once in that sacred space, they perform the core of the ritual. This is done in a variety of ways (see chapter IV for details). The purpose of the core is to effect some change in the participants. This is another transition "from one stage of being to another." Finally, at the end of the ritual, the participants make a transition from the sacred space as they prepare to return to their daily lives.

What Is Said

Abingdon mentions "utterances of sounds, chants, mantras, or prayers, and the recitation of myths or sacred history" as those things "said" during ritual (see chapter II). The interviewees in this study report the inclusion of sounds, chants, and readings of myths and women's spiritual history during their rituals. In addition, several interviewees said they sing during their rituals.

What Is Seen

Abingdon states: "The visual symbols used in ritual include color, shapes, vessels, food stuffs, and hosts of other combinations" (see chapter II). In women's ritual, visual objects are very significant. Among the most important aspects of women's ritual are pictures or figures of various goddesses or heroines. Some interviewees also report putting various objects of personal significance on their ritual altar.

The Context of Ritual: Symbolic Time and Space

Ritual Space

"Certain places take on specific importance in the ritual experience," according to *The Abingdon Dictionary*. Besides temples and churches, "a home, a cavern, a riverbank, the foot of a tree, or a hilltop may become meaningful contexts for ritual events" (see chapter II).

Most of the participants in this study said they rotate doing rituals in the members' homes. However, some said on occasion they may do a ritual on a hilltop or at the beach. Also, the largest group does their annual weekend ritual event at a campsite. According to *Abingdon*, all of these may be meaningful places for ritual.

Ritual Time

Abingdon states certain times may be more significant than others for performing rituals. Among those times, it lists "the solar year with its new year and equinoxes, the lunar cycle, . . . " (see chapter II). Two of the ritual groups in this study plan their rituals around the lunar cycles and around the equinoxes and solstices. The one group that meets annually, in the fall, reported they meet at that time because fall is significant for endings and beginnings. The other two groups do not meet according to any of these significant times. Rather, one meets weekly and the other meets biweekly.

Types of Ritual

The Abingdon Dictionary reports the following types of ritual:

- Corporate, domestic, personal rituals
- Rituals of healing
- Festivals
- Rites of Passage

(For a more in-depth description of these types of ritual, see chapter II.)

The most common type of ritual performed by the participants in this study are personal rituals. According to *Abingdon* these rituals are done: " . ... without a structured social context. Such rituals tend to be in places and times that have meaning in one's personal history and express the identity and needs of the person or individual."[1]

In this study, none of the interviewees reported strong differentiation regarding types of ritual. In fact, some of their rituals are made up of two or more types. For example, while most rituals are personal, the participants often incorporate elements of healing into their rituals.

Among the festival rituals, *Abingdon* reports two types: 1) theofests and 2) ecofests (see chapter II for the description of these festivals). While all groups report that the symbolism of various goddesses and heroines is significant in their rituals, no group reported specific rituals devoted to a certain goddess or heroine. Thus no group has theofests per se. However, two groups observe ecofests. These two groups specifically schedule rituals around the seasonal events of equinoxes and solstices.

Also, no group reported doing specific rites of passage. However, *Abingdon* observes that all rituals can be regarded as rites of passage in that they permit "social and personal passage from one mode of being to another."[2] This is indeed applicable to women's ritual. In fact, this is one of the significant experiences that occurs in women's ritual. It is this "passage from one mode of being to another" that allows for the change or transformation women experience in women's ritual. It is because of this transformation that many women participate in women's ritual.

Ritual Framework Conclusion

The Abingdon Dictionary of Living Religions presents four elements of ritual. These elements are:

- Identity and transformation
- What is done, said, and seen
- Symbolic time and space
- Types of ritual

The framework for this study was drawn from these elements of ritual.

The results of this study indicate that the five groups participating in this study incorporate all of these elements in their rituals.

Summary of the Study

This text explored the characteristics of women who participate in women's ritual groups in the Bay Area and the characteristics of the five women's ritual groups participating in this study. It also examined the characteristics of women's ritual and the growth prospects for women's ritual. Finally, this text examined whether there is a relationship between women's ritual and the women's movement.

Characteristics of Women in Ritual Groups

The results of this study indicate that most of the women participating in women's ritual are white and middle class. Most are between the ages of thirty and fifty. They are more likely to be unmarried than married and more likely to be childless than to have children. Also, they are likely to have a master's degree, be a professional in some type of human service occupation, and earn $20,000 to $30,000 per year.

Characteristics of the Ritual Groups

The five groups participating in this study vary considerably. The ritual groups range in size from six participants to over one hundred participants. The groups vary about when they meet, from one group that meets weekly to another group that meets annually to hold one large weekend event of women's ritual. The groups vary in their origin. One group evolved out of a workshop on women's ritual, while a couple of other groups grew out of a small group of women who wanted to try doing women's ritual together. Finally, one of the groups no longer exists. It disbanded in the fall of 1986 after three years of existence.

Characteristics of Women's Ritual

The results of this study show that women's ritual is made up of three main parts. The first part of women's ritual is creating a safe place or a sacred space for the participants to do their ritual. The second part of ritual involves activity that results in some type of change or transformation of the ritual participants. And the third part of women's ritual is an ending, which prepares participants to leave the sacred space.

The interviewees were asked what they experienced during the different parts of their rituals. A common experience during the first part, creating sacred space, was feeling a sense of community and of being in a safe place. During the second part, the core of the ritual, common experiences for the interviewees were feeling in touch with themselves, feeling empowered, and feeling they actually can make a change. Finally, during the ending of the ritual, the interviewees reported feeling a sense of completion and a transition to daily life.

While these three parts of women's ritual are common to all the groups participating in this study, the manner in which each part is performed varies greatly both within and among the five groups (see chapter IV).

The roots or sources for women's ritual include adapting spiritual traditions from other cultures. These cultures include Native American, East Indian, Polynesian, and the pre-Christian or Old Religion of Western Europe, sometimes referred to as Wicca. In addition, the participants in women's ritual draw on the writings of spiritual feminists and on their own creativity to develop their rituals. Another significant consideration is creating rituals that meet the needs of the participants.

Relationship to the Women's Movement

Thirty of the thirty-three questionnaire respondents identify themselves as feminist and eighteen respondents belong to one or more women's organizations. In addition, eight of the ten respondents who participated in the interview said they had, at some time, been active in the women's movement. Six of these eight maintain some activism, though most said they are much less active than they were in the past. Further, some interviewees specifically stated that they see women's spirituality and/or women's ritual as an evolution or "maturation" of the women's movement.

This suggests there is a link between women's ritual and the women's movement. Further support for this is the fact that feminist journals and magazines, including *Heresies, Chrysalis,* and *Ms.* have featured women's spirituality in one or more of their issues (see chapter II).

Growth Prospects for Women's Ritual

All thirty-three respondents in this study think women's ritual is growing. While they foresee some problems for women's ritual, both internally and externally, they remain optimistic that it will grow. Some interviewees said they continue to meet more and more women who are interested in women's ritual. Others said there is too much momentum for it not to grow. Still others said women's ritual meets needs for women that are not met elsewhere. These reasons suggest the growth prospects for women's ritual are quite strong.

APPENDICES

Appendix A

Cover Letter and Survey Questionnaire for This Study

November 1986

Dear Ritual Group Members,

I am a graduate student in Women's Studies at San Jose State University. I have participated in women's rituals for several years and have a special interest in women's ritual.

I am studying the characteristics of women's ritual in the Bay Area. Please help me by completing and returning the attached survey.

The survey will take no longer than ten minutes to complete. The names of all individuals and groups participating in this survey will be kept strictly confidential. Also, results of the survey will be made available to all who participate in the survey. If you'd like the results mailed to you, please list your name and address below.

Thank you for your time.

Sincerely,

Barbara J. DesMarais

To receive survey results, list your name and address:

Name_____

Address_____

_____

Women's Ritual Survey

Background Questions

1. Age   under 20____   20-30____   30-40____   40-50____
   50-60____   60-70____   over 70____

2. Ethnic Background_____

3. Occupation_____

4. Education (check highest level completed)
   Less than 12 years_____   High school diploma____
   Some college coursework____   Bachelor's degree____
   Master's degree_____   Ph.D._____

5. Annual income under $10,000_____
   $10,000-$20,000_____ $20,000-30,000_____
   $30,000-$40,000_____ $40,000-$50,000_____
   over $50,000_____

6. Is the above income (check one) your income
   only_____   your partner's income only_____
   combined family income_____

7. Marital Status   Unmarried_____ Married_____

8. Sexual Orientation_____

9. Do you have children? Yes_____ No_____

Ritual and Ritual Group Characteristics and Purpose

1. How did you learn about women's ritual? (check one)
   Friend_____ Educational class_____
   Book_____ Magazine/newspaper_____
   Newsletter/flyer_____ Radio_____
   Other (please specify)_____

2. How long have you been doing ritual?
   Years_____ Months_____

3. How long has your ritual group existed?
   Years_____ Months_____ Don't know_____

4. How many members are in your ritual group?_____

5. How frequently do you attend your group's ritual meetings? Seldom_____ Often_____
   Almost always_____

6. Ritual serves many purposes. Which of the following purposes does ritual serve for you? (check all that apply) Meets spiritual needs_____ Meets social needs_____ Meets healing or therapeutic needs_____ Other (please describe)_____

7. Do you talk about your ritual group with (check all that apply) Friends_____ Family_____
   Co-workers_____ Professional associates_____
   Acquaintances_____ Strangers_____ No one outside the ritual group_____

8. Did you ever belong to a Christian or Jewish religion?
   Yes_____ No_____

If yes, how would you describe your experience with that religion? (check one) very positive____ positive_____ neutral_____ negative_____ very negative_____

9. If yes (on #8), do you still belong? Yes_____   No____

10. Do you consider yourself a feminist? Yes_____ No_____

11. How long do you think you will continue to participate in women's ritual?_____

12. How frequently does your ritual group meet?_____

13. What determines when your group will meet?_____
    _____

14. Does your ritual group have a leader?
    Yes_____   No_____

15. If yes (on #14), is the same person the leader for every meeting? Yes_____No_____

16. Are you involved in any of the following? (check all that apply)   NOW_____   NWPC_____   OWL____ WILPF_____
    Please list any other organizations, committees or task forces that focus on women's issues that you belong to or are involved with_____

Prospects for Growth of Women's Ritual

1. Do you see women's ritual as a growing phenomenon?
   Yes_____ No_____
   a) If no, why not?_____
   _____
   b) If yes, why?_____
   _____
   c) If yes, what changes, if any, do you see in women's
      ritual as it grows?_____
      _____

If you have any comments about your ritual group that
you'd like to add, please write them here._____
_____

Would you be willing to participate in a personal interview to further discuss women's ritual?   yes_____
no_____
If yes, please list your name_____
and your phone number_____

Appendix B

Interview Schedule for This Study

I. Structure/Form

Introduction:
I'd like to begin this interview by asking some historical and background questions about your group.

1. Do you know how your ritual group came to be formed?
   yes_____   no_____
   If yes, please tell me about it.

2. Does your group have membership?
   yes_____   no_____
   a) If no, why not?

   b) If yes, what are the requirements for member-ship?

3. Does your group have any rules?
   yes_____   no_____
   a) If yes, what are they? (list)

   b) Are there any other rules? (list)

c) I'd like to read each rule back to you and have you tell me how closely each rule is followed or adhered to, okay?

d) Are there ever any exceptions (to adherence)?

[If not mentioned under "3. Rules" ask e) and f) next]

e) Does your group allow visitors to attend rituals? yes_____ no_____
   1) If no, why not?

   2) If yes, are visitors allowed to attend all rituals? Why or why not?

f) Does your group ever allow men to attend rituals? yes_____ no_____
   1) If yes, when?

   2) If no, why not?

4. When do you meet?

When do you meet?

What determines when you meet?

Where do you get together?

Please tell me, in as much detail as possible, what you do when you get together? (List what is done)

(Go back over list of each "done" and ask why done).

[If only one type of ritual is described, ask if there is more than one type of ritual or does the group have a variety of rituals. If more than one type, list above and ask person to describe in as much detail as possible.]

5. Are your rituals based on any traditions?
   yes_____ no_____

   a) If yes, please tell me about the traditions and how your rituals are connected to these traditions.

   b) If yes, are your rituals based on anything other than these traditions? yes_____ no_____

      If yes, on what else are your rituals based?

   c) If no (on #5), please explain the origins of your rituals or on what are your rituals based?

6. Do you have any rites of passage specifically related to being female? (ex. menarch, menstruation, pregnancy, childbirth, menopause?)
   yes_____ no_____

   If yes, please tell me about these rites of passage.

   Are there any other types of rites of passage that your ritual group practices?
   yes_____ no_____

   If yes, please tell me about these rites of passage.

7. Do you have rituals (other than the rites of passage mentioned above) with a theme specifically related to being female? (ex. kinship - mother, daughter, aunt, godmother, etc.)
   yes_____ no_____

If yes, please describe these rituals to me.

8. Do you do rituals with family members, alone, or with people other than your group, that are related to your involvement with women's ritual? (ex. blessing food, blessing the garden, etc?)

yes_____ no_____

If yes, please tell me about these rituals.

Are there any other ceremonies or rituals you do in your home that are connected to women's ritual?

yes_____ no_____

If yes, would you describe these for me?

9. How does your group make decisions?

[If not answered by above question, ask the following:] Are your group decisions made by all or most participants or are your group's decisions made by a few participants? (i.e., who participates in decision-making?)

10. Some groups differ in their structure. Some groups have leaders. Some give individual members certain responsibilities that rotate while others have more permanent responsibilities. Would you please tell me how your group is organized. (List below).

Responsibilities	Length of Term	Basis for assignment (volunteer, voted in, etc.)

11. Some groups indicate one of their bigger issues is interpersonal conflict.

   a) What, if any, process does your group use to deal with interpersonal conflicts?

   b) How effective is this process in resolving interpersonal conflicts?

   c) If no process, why is there no process? (Is conflict not dealt with?)

II. Belief System/Values

Introduction:
Now that we've talked about the history of your group and about what you do when you get together, I'd like to talk about what these things mean to you.

1. First, I would like to understand what you experience when you do ritual. We've talked about the different kinds of rituals that your group does. Perhaps some rituals are different from other rituals, for you.

   [Then pick out one ritual from the list (I.4) and ask: "What do you experience when you do this ritual?"]

   [Probe—"Can you tell me more about that, etc."]

   [Then pick out another ritual, ask if different, and if so, how? Do this till all rituals and the experiences of each are listed.]

2. Is there a set of "beliefs" that everyone in your group shares?
   yes_____   no_____

   a) If no, why not?

   b) If yes, what are they?

3. Is there a set of "values" that everyone in your group shares? yes_____   no_____

   a) If no, why not?

   b) If yes, what are they?

4. Does your ritual group have a common definition of right and wrong or good and bad?
   yes_____   no_____

   If no, why not?

   If yes, can you give me that "common definition"?

5. Are there any rituals addressing wrongs?
   yes_____   no_____

   If yes, please describe.

   Are there any other methods than ritual of addressing wrongs?
   yes_____   no_____

   If yes, please describe.

6. Sometimes women's ritual groups are called women's spiritual groups or women's spirituality groups. I'd like to know if you would describe your group as a spiritual group–but first I need your definition of "spiritual." How would you define spiritual?

   Would you describe your group as a spiritual group?
   yes_____ no_____
   Why or why not?

7. Now I'd like to ask whether or not you would define your group as a religious group–but first I need your definition of "religious." How would you define religious?

   Would you describe your group as a religious group?
   yes_____ no_____
   Why or why not?

III. Growth Potential

1. Do you think your group is getting stronger or weaker or staying about the same? (circle one)

   a) Why?

   b) Do you have new members joining, old members dropping out or both? (circle one)

      Has your group size increased, decreased, or stayed about the same? (circle one)

c) Are you meeting more frequently, less frequently, or about the same? (circle one)

d) Are you creating more new rituals?
yes_____ no_____

2. What do you think will happen to your group:

    a) In the next two years?

    b) In the next five years?

3. How is your ritual group made known and available to women in your area?

4. Let's shift our focus from your particular group and look at the women's ritual movement as a whole. Do you think the women's ritual group movement is likely to grow or stay about the same? (circle one)

    Why or why not (grow)? (List reasons).

    [Go over list. Probe for positives if only negatives are listed and vice versa].

    a) So you think the reasons women's ritual will grow are: (go over above list)

       Can you add more reasons why you think women's ritual will grow or any other strengths of women's ritual?

    b) So you think the reasons women's ritual may not grow are: (go over above list)

Can you add any more reasons why you think
women's ritual may not grow or any other problems with women's ritual?

5. For what reasons do you think some groups fail to
continue?

6. How many other women's ritual groups in the San
Francisco Bay Area are you aware of?

How did you choose your group?

IV. Relationship of Women's Ritual to the Women's Movement

1. I'm interested in whether you would define yourself as
a feminist, so could you first tell me how you would
define a feminist?

By your definition, do you consider yourself a feminist?

2. Were you ever socially or politically active in any
aspects of the women's movement?
yes_____   no_____

a) If yes, what groups or causes did you participate
in or in what ways were you active?

Are you still active?
yes_____   no_____
Why or why not?

96

a) If no, did you have a conscious reason for not participating?
yes_____ no_____

If yes, what were the reasons?

That's all the questions I have. Thank you for your time and your participation. I hope to have the survey results compiled by early spring and I will send copies of the results at that time. Again, thank you for participating in this interview.

Endnotes

I. Introduction

1. G. A. and A. G. Theodorson, *A Modern Dictionary of Sociology* (New York: Thomas J. Crowell, Co., 1969), 39.
2. Anne Kent Rush, *Moon, Moon* (New York: Random House, 1976), 333.
3. From *The Abingdon Dictionary of Living Religions*, ed. Keith Crim. Copyright ©1981 by Abingdon. (Nashville: Abingdon, 1981), 624. Used by permission.

II. Review of Related Literature

1. Merlin Stone, *When God Was a Woman* (New York: Harcourt Brace Jovanovich, 1976), 61.
2. M.J. Gage, *Woman, Church and State* (New York: Arno Press, 1972), 247.
3. Carol P. Christ and Judith Plaskow, *Womanspirit Rising* (San Francisco: Harper & Row, 1979), 124.
4. ibid., pp. 120–30.
5. ibid., p. 286.
6. Kay Turner, "Contemporary Feminist Rituals," in *The Politics of Women's Spirituality*, ed. C. Spretnak (Garden City: Anchor Press/Doubleday, 1982), 222.
7. ibid., p. 227.
8. ibid., p. 226.
9. ibid., p. 226.
10. ibid., p. 231.
11. ibid., p. 227.
12. ibid., p. 232.
13. Hallie Iglehart, *Womanspirit* (San Francisco: Harper & Row, 1983), 123.
14. ibid., p. 124.
15. ibid., p. 126.

16. Charlene Spretnak, ed., *The Politics of Women's Spirituality* (Garden City: Anchor Press/Doubleday, 1982), xxi.
17. Paula Gunn Allen, *The Sacred Hoop: Rediscovering the Feminine in American Indian Traditions* (Boston: Beacon Press, 1985), 195.
18. Allen, pp. 79–80.
19. From *The Abingdon Dictionary of Living Religions* ed. Keith Crim. Copyright ©1981 by Abingdon. (Nashville: Abingdon, 1981), 624. Used by permission.
20. ibid., p. 624.
21. ibid., p. 624.
22. ibid., p. 624.
23. ibid., p. 625.
24. ibid., p. 625.
25. ibid., p. 625.
26. ibid., p. 625.
27. ibid., p. 626.
28. ibid., p. 626.
29. ibid., p. 626.
30. ibid., p. 626.
31. ibid., pp. 626–7.
32. ibid., p. 627.
33. ibid., p. 627.

IV. Results and Discussion

1. Kay Turner, "Contemporary Feminist Rituals," in *The Politics of Women's Spirituality*, ed. C. Spretnak (Garden City: Anchor Press/Doubleday, 1982), 227.

V. Conclusion

1. From *The Abingdon Dictionary of Living Religions*, ed. Keith Crim. Copyright ©1981 by Abingdon. (Nashville: Abingdon, 1981), p. 626.
2. ibid., p. 627.

Bibliography

Literature influencing this study though not necessarily referenced in this text.

Adler, Margot. *Drawing Down the Moon.* Boston: Beacon Press, 1979.

Allen, Paula Gunn. *The Sacred Hoop: Recovering the Feminine in American Indian Traditions.* Boston: Beacon Press, 1985.

Bolen, Jean Shinoda, M.D. *Goddesses in Everywoman.* San Francisco: Harper and Row, 1984.

Bradley, Marion Zimmer. *The Mists of Avalon.* New York: Alfred A. Knopf, 1983.

Budapest, Zsuzsana E. *The Holy Book of Women's Mysteries: Part I.* Los Angeles: Susan B. Anthony Coven No. 1, 1979.

———. *The Holy Book of Women's Mysteries: Part II.* Los Angeles: Susan B. Anthony Coven No. 1, 1979.

———. *The Rise of the Fates.* Los Angeles: Susan B. Anthony Coven No. 1, 1976.

Caldecott, Leonie, and Stephanie Leland, eds. *Reclaim the Earth.* London: The Women's Press Limited, 1983.

Cameron, Anne. *Daughters of Copper Woman.* Vancouver, B.C.: Press Gang Publishers, 1981.

Carson, Anne. *Feminist Spirituality and the Feminine Divine: An Annotated Bibliography.* Trumansburg, N.Y.: The Crossing Press, 1985.

Christ, Carol P., and Judith Plaskow, eds. *Womanspirit Rising.* San Francisco: Harper and Row, 1979.

Crim, K., ed. *Abingdon Dictionary of Living Religions.* Nashville: Abingdon, 1981.

Daly, Mary. *Beyond God the Father.* Boston: Beacon Press, 1973.

———. *Gyn/Ecology.* Boston: Beacon Press, 1978.

Durdin-Robertson, Lawrence. *Juno Covella Perpetual Calendar of the Fellowship of Isis*. Enniscorthy, Eire: The Nationalist & Leinster Times, Ltd., 1982.

Dworkin, Andrea. *Woman Hating*. New York: Dutton, 1974.

Evans, Arthur. *Witchcraft and the Gay Counterculture*. Boston: Fag Rag Books, 1978.

French, Marilyn. *Beyond Power*. New York: Summit Books, 1985.

Gage, Matilda Joslyn. *Woman, Church and State*. New York: Arno Press, 1972.

Gimbutas, Marija. *The Gods and Goddesses of Old Europe*. Berkeley: University of California Press, 1974.

Hall, Nor. *The Moon and the Virgin*. New York: Harper and Row, 1980.

Iglehart, Hallie. *Womanspirit*. San Francisco: Harper and Row, 1983.

Mariechild, Diane. *Mother Wit*. Trumansburg, N.Y.: The Crossing Press, 1981.

McAllister, Pam, ed. *Reweaving the Web of Life*. Philadelphia: New Society Publishers, 1982.

Morgan, Elaine. *The Descent of Woman*. New York: Bantam books, Inc., 1972.

Morgan, Robin. *Going Too Far*. New York: Vintage Books, 1978.

————. *Sisterhood Is Global*. Garden City, N.Y.: Anchor Press/Doubleday, 1984.

Mountaingrove, Jean and Ruth, eds. *Womanspirit* 1–40, Fall 1975–Summer 84.

Murray, Margaret A. *The God of the Witches*. London: Sampson Low, Marston and Co., Ltd., 1931: reprint ed., Oxford: Oxford University Press, 1970.

————. *The Witch-Cult in Western Europe*. Oxford: Oxford University Press, 1921: reprint ed., 1971.

Myerhoff, Barbara. "Rites of Passage: Process and Paradox." In *Celebration: Studies in Festival and Ritual*. Victor Turner, ed., Washington, D.C.: Smithsonian Institution Press, 1982.

Neihardt, John C. *Black Elk Speaks*. Lincoln: University of Nebraska Press, Lincoln, 1961.

Noble, Vicki. *Motherpeace*. San Francisco: Harper and Row, 1983.

Piercy, Marge. *Woman on the Edge of Time.* New York: Fawcett Crest, 1976.

Rank, Shirley A. *Cakes for the Queen of Heaven.* Boston: Dept. of Religious Education, Unitarian Universalist Assoc., 1985.

Rohrlich, Ruby, and Elaine Hoffman Baruch, eds. *Women in Search of Utopia.* New York: Schochen Books, 1984.

Rush, Anne Kent. *Moon, Moon.* New York: Random House, 1976.

Schaef, Anne Wilson. *Women's Reality.* Minneapolis: Winston Press, Inc., 1981.

Spretnak, Charlene. *Lost Goddesses of Early Greece.* Boston: Beacon Press, 1978.

Spretnak, Charlene, ed. *The Politics of Women's Spirituality.* Garden City: Anchor Press/Doubleday, 1982.

Starhawk. *Dreaming the Dark.* Boston: Beacon Press, 1981.

———. *The Spiral Dance.* San Francisco: Harper and Row, 1979.

Stein, Diane. *The Kuan Yin Book of Changes.* St. Paul: Llewellyn Publications, 1985.

Steinem, Gloria, ed. *Ms.* (December 1985).

Stone, Merlin. *When God Was a Woman.* New York: Harcourt Brace Jovanovich, 1976.

Tatelbaum, Judy. *The Courage to Grieve.* New York: Harper and Row, 1980.

Teish, Luisah. *Jambalaya: The Natural Woman's Book of Personal Charms and Practical Rituals.* San Francisco: Harper and Row, 1985.

Theodorson, G. A. and A. G. *A Modern Dictionary of Sociology.* New York: Thomas J. Crowell, 1969.

Turner, Kay. "Contemporary Feminist Rituals." In *The Politics of Women's Spirituality*, Charlene Spretnak, ed. Garden City: Anchor Press/Doubleday, 1982.

Turner, Victor. *Dramas, Fields, and Metaphors.* Ithaca: Cornell University Press, 1974.

———. *The Ritual Process: Structure and Anti-Structure.* Ithaca: Cornell University Press, 1969: reprint ed., 1985.

Van Sertima, Ivan. *Black Women in Antiquity.* New Brunswick: Transaction Books, 1985.

Walker, Barbara G. *The Crone*. San Francisco: Harper and Row, 1985.

———. *The Woman's Encyclopedia of Myths and Secrets*. San Francisco: Harper and Row, 1979.

Weinstein, Marion. *Positive Magic*. Custer, WA: Phoenix Publishing, 1981.